Ten-Minute Scriptural, Earthy Sermons for the Contemporary Scene

Ten-Minute, Scriptural, Earthy Sermons for the Contemporary Scene

With Discussion Questions

NOEL W. DAVIS

RESOURCE *Publications* • Eugene, Oregon

TEN-MINUTE, SCRIPTURAL, EARTHY SERMONS FOR THE CONTEMPORARY SCENE
With Discussion Questions

Copyright © 2024 Noel W. Davis. All rights reserved. Except for brief quotations in critical publications or reviews, no part of this book may be reproduced in any manner without prior written permission from the publisher. Write: Permissions, Wipf and Stock Publishers, 199 W. 8th Ave., Suite 3, Eugene, OR 97401.

Resource Publications
An Imprint of Wipf and Stock Publishers
199 W. 8th Ave., Suite 3
Eugene, OR 97401

www.wipfandstock.com

PAPERBACK ISBN: 979-8-3852-0766-4
HARDCOVER ISBN: 979-8-3852-0767-1
EBOOK ISBN: 979-8-3852-0768-8

01/17/24

Cover design—Mike Surber—Photo supplied by Scott Thompson

The church was originally Graceville Methodist, then Graceville Uniting. It is a Gothic structure in concrete opened in 1929. It was designed and built by Walter Taylor, 1872–1955—who is Noel Davis's grandfather. It is sometimes referred to as "the suburban cathedral."

Noel Davis grew up in this church, being active in its many relevant groups till he was 19 when he began training for the Methodist ministry.

To the ongoing Church.
With thanks to: Graceville Methodist (Uniting),
Somerville House, Jacaranda Street Uniting Church (Trinity).

Contents

Preface | ix
Keep it Simple | 1
Illness and Misfortune—They Happen | 4
Possibilities and Responsibilities | 8
A Matter of the Heart | 12
All Being Well | 16
Wearing Justice | 20
Hope and Life | 23
Saving the Message | 27
A Pivotal Decision | 31
Jesus bids us Shine | 35
More than Sufficient | 39
Individual Worth | 43
Jesus and People | 47
New Beginnings | 51
Following the Leader, Jesus | 55
Jesus and Healing | 59
Unlimited Compassion | 63
The Pluses of Being Children | 67
Sleepless in Ipswich | 71
Growing Towards Integrity | 75

Contents

Top Priority | 79
Repentance is the Way to Go | 83
A Searching but Honest View of Self | 87
The Lord's Supper | 91
Let's Celebrate | 95
The Stuff of Life | 99
It's Love, Love, Love | 103
The Church Uniting | 107
Prophets All | 111
A Vital Balance | 115
Jesus's People | 119
Be Good | 123
Jesus Crucified | 127
The Essential Guide to Worthwhile Living | 131
Afterword: The Art of Preaching | 135

Preface

Very few people would list preaching with the "arts" but the afterword titled "The Art of Preaching" wants to suggest that there are certain skills involved in fulfilling the role in a worthwhile manner. I started preaching when I was 16 and am now 91. The early start was due to my father who was a Methodist local preacher and gave me the opportunity to do the sermon in one of his services. Before and during my training to be a Methodist, then Uniting Church minister I carried out a great deal of preaching, indeed I still preach each month.

Preaching has a long and wide tradition. I'm aware that Jesus, some 2000 years ago preached in a Synagogue in Nazareth and that preaching was a tradition in Judaism, and that passed on to Christianity. I'm aware that preaching forms a definite part of Islam and discovered that preaching has a meaning in a number of languages such as Tamil and Hindi.

It may have been a surprise to some who have at least read the title of this book to see that it purports to contain "10 minute sermons." Some current congregations feel cheated if the sermon is less than three quarters of an hour and there was a time in English churches when there were people roaming a congregation with the responsibility of waking up congregational members who had lapsed into sleep. For the last 11 years of my ministry I was chaplain in a Uniting and Presbyterian church girls school. I preached almost countless sermons in Assemblies, Chapel and boarder's

Preface

services. When I took up the role, it was with the notion that 15 minutes was a good length for any sermon. Although the students were not openly rude I soon realised that 10 minutes was a maximal length for a sermon if there was to be any hope of gaining attention. After retiring from active ministry I have continued the practice of preaching for 10 minutes. Rarely are there complaints.

The sermons contained in this book are all based on verses or passages of the Bible. Hence the use of "Scriptural" in the title. This is not the place to speak of varying attitudes towards the Bible amongst Christians but without exception the various denominations within Christianity give prominent place to the Bible. It is my firm belief that the Bible as a whole and particularly the gospels, setting out the life, teaching and attitudes of Jesus has a great deal to offer contemporary society but many times needs interpretation and varying emphasis, hence this book. I included the word "earthy" in the title following Scriptural to make the point that every effort is made in the following sermons to apply the Biblical words to contemporary, everyday life.

The only other comment which I feel needs to be made in connection with this Preface is to do with "discussion questions." Occasionally over the years in smaller congregations I have adopted the practice of having a discussion question after each point of the sermon. There have been favourable comments about the practice. Since these sermons are of 10 minute length, it is my hope that they could lend themselves to use with discussion groups.

2 Kings 5: 1–17—The story of Naaman the Syrian General who has some sort of skin disease. A captured Jewish girl suggests that he goes to Samaria to a prophet there to be cured. When he gets to Elisha's place the prophet doesn't even come out to see him and suggests he bathes seven times in the Jordan River. He is outraged at the suggestion as he was expecting something spectacular and wants to storm off but his servants dissuade him suggesting he should not let himself be deterred.

Keep it Simple

INTRODUCTION

We're using part of this story to consider the idea of "Keeping it Simple." Even though earlier translations suggest that Naaman had leprosy, it is probably the case that he had a variety of skin disease. (Tell the story as above).

A SIMPLE FAITH

So let's consider faith or the entry into the Christian life. Over the years on a number of occasions I've heard people described as having a simple faith usually meaning that they don't engage in a lot of questioning and their faith has lasted through testing experiences. I started training for the ministry through Home Missionary Training College for 12 months and then spent time at North Rockhampton and Pomona. Before I headed for King's College a number of people said to me and I know a number of other ministers had the same experience, don't let College change you. I think I know what people meant, that it could be possible to go through 3 or 4 years of college, and come out with one's head in the clouds or perhaps being too absorbed in the various fields of study covered such as Theology, Biblical Studies, Philosophy and all the rest.

It would be unfortunate if we felt that when it comes to the Christian faith, we should switch off our minds and be completely unquestioning. Young people in more recent years have been encouraged to question what is presented to them in education and to form their own opinions. The Christian faith should be able to stand up to questioning and testing and I believe there are some parts of traditional belief which are rather misleading—such as feeling that everything that happens has to be accepted as God's will and Jesus's death on the cross was necessary for our salvation. Then there are questions such as why do bad things happen to good people. I believe that it is all important that the core of belief be simple. The core is to respond as the early disciples did to the call of Jesus to follow him so that we seek to follow the way of Jesus as we move through life.

THE HELPS AND HINDRANCES OF RITUAL

The second point is really sparked off by Naaman's request that he take home some soil from Samaria so he could worship the God of Israel. Elisha said that it wasn't necessary. To me it raises the question of ritual, how we go about worship. The different approaches to how we go about worship across the various Christian denominations are amazing from the more elaborate forms such as in the Catholic, Orthodox and Anglican churches to the approach of the Quakers which is largely silent. We grow accustomed to certain forms of worship and what we do becomes ritual. We can even become attached to where we sit in church. Some more recent churches may suggest that in their modern approaches they are avoiding ritual but if they follow, basically, the same procedure they are establishing ritual. We can't really avoid ritual and we need it as there is something comforting and familiar about what we do from Sunday to Sunday. It was interesting when the Roman Catholic Church decided to use English rather than Latin in the Mass so people could understand what was being said. There was a strong move from some Catholic people in objection as the Latin Mass had become familiar. Ritual becomes a hindrance if we maintain that what we do is the right and only way.

Keep it Simple

LIFE IS SIMPLY WONDERFUL

In this final point as the heading suggests I want to apply the "Keep it Simple" principle to life in general, to recognise that life is "simply wonderful." I'm thinking of the huge variety of forms of life from the microscopic to the huge such as the elephant and the whale. To wake up each morning to the twittering of birds—to walk by the sea. The process of meeting someone to whom we are attracted and discovering that the feeling is mutual and so the start of a relationship. Of course, when we analyse life, the earth and the universe, it is hugely complex and there is so much we do not yet understand. Also, of course, life can be difficult and tragic and this is unavoidable at some stage. Individuals can be resilient and support is generally available. It's amazing how some people who face handicaps come to accept them and learn to adapt. We have a friend who was born with no arms. She has learnt to do most things with her feet. When we first met her on Lamb Island and invited her and her husband for a meal, it was a while before we realised that she was holding her fork between her toes to eat, as it was all done with so little fuss.

So, I believe, Naaman the Syrian has led us to a very important principle—"Keep it Simple."

QUESTIONS

1. What do you regard as basic Christian faith? Is there some aspect you regard as essential? Why? Is there such a thing as an individual approach to faith?
2. What parts of church ritual would you miss most if for some reason the approach you are familiar with was discontinued?
3. What brings about the most wonder for you in the earth, its creatures, relationships, day to day life?

Job 42:4-6—"You told me to listen and answer your questions. I heard about you from others; now I have seen you with my own eyes. That's why I hate myself and sit here in dust and ashes to show my sorrow."

Illness and Misfortune—They Happen

INTRODUCTION

I've indicated a couple of verses from Job as our text but really this sermon is an effort to put the book of Job into the long history of people seeking to understand "pain, misfortune and loss" and how they relate to faith.

LIFE IS FRAGILE

The earth teems with life from the smallest bacteria, virus, and insect to the mammoth blue whale. Every time we take a step we are almost certainly treading on a number of near microscopic creatures. This is why a sect of the Hindus, the Jains, have someone sweep the paths ahead of them in an effort to avoid killing anything unnecessarily. I think this is extreme but I do try to avoid stomping on or swatting anything that doesn't by nature cause harm. The higher one goes in intelligence and understanding the more problematic the fragility of life seems to become. It's great to wake up each morning to bird song and it provides a cheerful backdrop to the day but the birds are behaving like that because they are hard wired to do so. They don't have to stop to think will I sing happily right now. There's no doubt that the other animals feel pain and there are examples of elephants for example showing grief at the loss of a calf. Since we are capable of thought and reasoning and with a wide range of emotions it is understandable that humankind has wrestled with the why of pain and loss. Going back to the

Illness and Misfortune—They Happen

heading of this point, life is fragile and pain is a part of life. There are simple answers to the question why pain? If we didn't feel pain we wouldn't know to withdraw our hand from something that is hot or realise that we had suffered some sort of injury or illness. Because we become attached to loved ones and friends, and enjoy company and companionship when they are withdrawn from us through age, illness or accident we suffer the pain of loss and grief. Those are the answers staring us in the face.

BELIEVERS STRUGGLE WITH ILLNESS AND MISFORTUNE

We're turning now far more directly to the issues dealt with in Job. I believe there's a growth in understanding of how pain and misfortune relate to faith as we follow through the Bible. In the early parts of the Bible there is a direct relation between people's behaviour and particularly their attitude to God and what happens in their life and the life of the community. If, for example, the Israelites were going into battle and they lost, then it was immediately thought that situation came about because of their misbehaviour or lack of faith. In Job there is further exploration. The fallen angel Satan gets permission from God to bring all sorts of misfortune to Job who has been a prime example of a righteous and faithful individual to test him out. The suggestion is that sickness and misfortune and loss could be the work of evil. We then move to Jesus himself. He shows a willingness to heal people, and therefore a concern and compassion for illness and loss. There are two things he said in this regard which are particularly helpful. One is recorded in Luke 2. Jesus had been told that Pilate had given orders for some people from Galilee to be killed, while they were offering sacrifices. He asked if people thought they were worse sinners than anyone else because of what had happened and gave an emphatic no. Then on another occasion recorded in Matthew 5 he stated that "God sends his rain on the just and the unjust. In other words misfortune and illness are completely random. Certainly if someone continues to smoke in

Illness and Misfortune—They Happen

spite of the warnings they could well suffer the consequences and this would be true of someone having an accident while driving after drinking alcohol. Also there is obviously a direct cause of suffering and death as a result of the use of various weapons in a conflict situation.

DEALING WITH ILLNESS AND MISFORTUNE

In this last point I want to consider actually dealing with illness and misfortune in the course of life. It is probably almost inescapable to ask, "why should this happen to me/." As we've just indicated there is no easy answer. If someone should ask that question glib answers are not the way to go. It may not bring immediate comfort but at some stage it has to be said, there is no answer. The most worthwhile question to be asked is, "how?" how can I deal with this? We're fortunate to be living when we do with the huge advances made and still being made in medical science. It's important to allow people to work through their attitudes rather than imposing one's own ideas. When it comes to long term illness or handicaps of varying descriptions, there are two steps needed neither necessarily easy—acceptance and adaptation. As followers of Jesus we follow someone who himself went through incredible suffering and we are a part of a church which as the body of Christ partly exists to provide active concern and support.

QUESTIONS

1. While injury and/or illness are not inevitable it is unlikely for any individual to avoid them. Is this something we can prepare for?

2. People of faith have wrestled with the fact that misfortune may happen to anyone whatever their religious belief. When misfortune strikes what help, if any, is belief?

3. Do you think the approach suggested in Point 3 to deal with injury, disability and/or loss makes sense? How difficult could the two steps of acceptance and adaptation be?

Psalm 8:3-9—Verse 5: "You made us a little lower than the angels."

Possibilities and Responsibilities

INTRODUCTION

I consider this is a remarkable Psalm. One has to realise it was probably written down in about 500 BC after having been passed on orally for centuries. I was the Chaplain at Somerville House, a Uniting and Presbyterian church girls' school of over 1000 for 11 years. As a School Chaplain I made a point of going on all the camps at the various Year levels. I think it was Year 11's who for a few years had their camp on South Stradbroke Island. One of my roles was to have brief devotions at the end of the day. On North Stradbroke I would ask the students to go to part of the island away from the lights of the camp. I would ask them to lie down so they could look at the stars and did so myself and would recite the words of this Psalm with a brief follow up.

THE UNIVERSE AND US

While there was an advantage for all of us at the camp gazing at the stars being on an Island, the lights of the Gold Coast were not far away. The Psalmist had a huge advantage in looking up at the night sky in a day when there were probably oil lamps. There is an incredible difference in what one is able to see in the night sky between looking up maybe way out West from looking up around here. Personally, I can never get my head around what is involved in the universe. I can never remember even the following brief details. "A single light year is 9.5 trillion kilometres. The distance light travels in one year. Light travels through space at 300,000 kilometres per second. The largest known star in our galaxy, Eta Carinae, 7,500 light years distant is 400 times the size of the sun and 4 million times as bright. There are 200–400 billion stars in our galaxy. There are 100 million galaxies and 3 septillion stars in the universe, a septillion is one plus 24–42 zeroes. That just gives further substance to the feelings of the Psalmist, against that immensity each of us is a mere pin prick.

OUR POSSIBILITIES

But there's more, for the Psalmist went on to say in relation to God, "but you made us a little lower than the angels" or some translations have, "a little lower than a god." Wow, one might say. Remember the writer of Genesis, probably writing about the same time as this Psalm, said that human beings are made in God's image. There's at least another sermon in that quote but you see the appropriateness of the heading of this point, Our Possibilities. Perhaps it would be better put to be, our infinite possibilities. Biologically we share most of the functions of the other animals and we are human animals. We do have greater dexterity than many others thanks to our hands and fingers. The biggest difference is the size of our brains or the complexity of them This isn't, of course, a biology lesson so I won't go into more detail but will list our possibilities. Powers of thought and reasoning, creativity in a great number of areas, decision making and goal setting ability, powers of communication and to form beliefs, a huge range of emotions with the peak being love. When Jesus issued the challenge to people, "follow me" it was a challenge to make maximal use of these possibilities in seeking to follow the way of life he set down.

OUR RESPONSIBILITIES

There's a passage in Matthew 20 which recounts the mother of the disciples, James and John asking Jesus if her sons could sit on the

POSSIBILITIES AND RESPONSIBILITIES

right and left of Jesus when he came into his kingdom. It shows a complete misunderstanding of Jesus's intentions in his mission. Jesus eventually says in his reply, "if you want to be first you must be the slave of all the rest." In other words, serving others should be the top of anybody's agenda if they want to have worthwhile lives. I want to put that with some words of the Psalmist we're focussing on, he's speaking of humankind, "You let us rule everything your hands have made." He then goes on to spell out how humankind have dominance over all living creatures. I spoke earlier of the size and complexity of the human brain which has meant that over the centuries, human kind, in general, has dominated and many times exploited the other forms of life and that has also often been to their and the planet's detriment. The heading of this point is our responsibilities which is why I started it by stressing our need to be ready to serve. I believe the Psalmist got it right with the place human kind has amongst all living things but it also means that we have responsibility for looking to the well-being of it all. There's at least one more sermon as a follow up but not now. There are good signs that across the earth people are waking up to the need to take much, much more care with the earth and its creatures. The message of the Psalm is that each of us have great possibilities, above all a worthwhile place in life but that includes a willingness to serve and we do it best as we seek to follow the way of Jesus. Amen

QUESTIONS

1. Do you think planet earth is the only one in the universe supporting life? b. Do you think humankind should seek to inhabit other planets?

2. Over the centuries, at times, there has been a great emphasis on the need for human individuals to have excessive humility or denigrate themselves. Do you consider this is a mistake in the light of statements such as this one of the Psalmist, that human beings are "a little lower than the angels?" b. Does

Possibilities and Responsibilities

the Christian message make enough of the wide potential of every individual?

3. There is no doubt that Jesus saw his role in the world as one of service and challenged everyone who follows him to do the same. What forms of service are you or could you be involved in? b. Do you think the church as a whole, takes really seriously the needs of the total environment? Is this an important avenue of service for any follower of Jesus?

Psalm 40:8 "I enjoy pleasing you. Your law is in my heart"

A Matter of the Heart

INTRODUCTION

In the season of Epiphany in the Christian year we remember that Jesus was made known to the whole world as illustrated by the three Magi or "wise men" coming from the East to celebrate the coming of Jesus. Our text doesn't mention other nations or diverse peoples but the simple and direct words set out a worthwhile message for all.

WITH ALL ONE'S HEART

The Psalmist wrote "your law is in my heart." What did he mean as he wrote the words some 2500 years ago. To the ancient Jews the heart was the source of all life's physical, intellectual, emotional, and will energies. They weren't, it seems, aware of its actual physical function. They were aware of their hearts beating faster at times depending on their situation which is why we can have the theme which we do this morning, "A Matter of the Heart" Donald Soper was a prominent Methodist minister in England of some decades ago who did a lot of open-air preaching. On one occasion he was challenging his hearers to give their hearts to Jesus. One feller who was probably a little better dressed than the others said, "Your heart is just a pump." Soper replied, I suppose you're going to say to your girl later on tonight, "I love you with all my pump." With the development of medical knowledge, we're very aware of the function of our hearts in keeping us alive and that it doesn't have to stop beating for long to cause our death but because of its reaction in pleasant and dangerous situations we use the word many times to express our responses, so we can speak of something being "heart felt" or doing something "with all one's heart." The Psalmist was saying that God's law or what God wanted was very much a part of his life and his intentions. I have to say that over the years I've avoided the use of phrases such as "letting Jesus into your heart" with children and young people. I prefer to use words such as, putting Jesus and his way central in one's life or just being committed to following Jesus.

ENJOYING DOING WHAT GOD WANTS

I think it was this part of the verse which took my attention "I enjoy pleasing you." If someone asks us what we enjoy doing or what's our favourite thing. I doubt if we would say, at least straight off, "pleasing God." We'll give a bit more thought a little later to "what God wants" but I think seeking to please God, or doing what God wants or following Jesus is the foundation of everything else. It gives us overall purpose and everything else involved in life fits into that or is built on it. I think sometimes people seeking to follow Jesus have misunderstood what is necessary and their lives have been less than enjoyable. We can think of devout people living in isolation at times in History or causing themselves pain in various ways or starving themselves. I'm not sure God is necessarily impressed. On one occasion when dealing with this issue Jesus used what seemed to be a game as an illustration, "You people are like children sitting in the market and shouting to each other. "We played the flute, but you wouldn't dance! We sang a funeral song, but you wouldn't mourn." He then pointed out that John the Baptist lived the life of a hermit and people thought he had a devil, but Jesus went around eating and drinking like any other person and people said, he eats and drinks too much. I think the answer is everything in moderation but people are making a mistake if they feel that they are pleasing Jesus by withdrawing from enjoyment in life. When someone has a life changing experience, may be in a church service, through some crisis in their lives, through reading a book, or through a discussion, they will often feel exhilarated and that's great but it just isn't possible to stay on that sort of high but it is possible to feel contented with one's course of action and that one is leading a worthwhile life.

JUST WHAT DOES GOD WANT

The Psalmist partly answers this question in earlier verses by saying what he feels God does not want, "Sacrifices and offerings are not what please you; gifts and payment for sin are not what you demand." It took a long time for the system of offering various sacrifices of animals at the temple to be given up. It was still in effect in the days of Jesus. It's not the acts designed to appease God or earn his favour which count but as set out in other passages how people are treated, being honest in business being concerned about those in need. Jesus very clearly set out towards the end of his life the standards by which the worthwhileness of a life is assessed with attention being paid to those who have various physical needs. Jesus made the point that in doing something for someone in need we are, in effect, doing it to him. The message, I believe, is not that we give up worship and our giving but that we allow its stimulation and opportunities to prepare us for worthwhile life from day to day. The Psalmist obviously felt that the chief way he could be pleasing to God was by loving the law. I'm not sure if the Psalmist meant all the laws which fill the early books of the Bible which cover various rituals and approaches to life. I'm sure that is most unhelpful to us but Jesus set those who want to follow him on the right track when he said that the most important commandments are those about love, love to God, love to people, measured by love for ourselves and for other people seeking to follow Jesus. It's the core of a worthwhile life and can occupy us for the whole of life. Amen

A Matter of the Heart

QUESTIONS

1. Do you share the writer's aversion to the expression, "having Jesus in your heart" if so, why? If you don't, why is it important to you?

2. Why do you think some people sincerely seeking to follow Jesus feel that they have to mostly show it by avoiding what often brings enjoyment to others e.g. social drinking, dancing, any others?

3. Do you think Point 3 adequately sets out what God wants? If you were asked, what course do you think God would most want someone to follow, what would you answer? Do you think following the way of Jesus is the way to get maximal value from life and give maximal value to it?

Psalm 90:17 "Our Lord and our God, treat us with kindness and let all go well for us. Please let all go well."

All Being Well

INTRODUCTION

The last verse of this Psalm really grabbed my attention, "Please let all go well." It reminded me very much of my mother who would always add "all being well" to any statement of future plans, so, "we'll leave for Burleigh Heads on such and such a date, all being well." I guess it's a version of "God willing."

FACING UNCERTAINTY

We live with uncertainty. We wake up any morning, and I'm assuming everyone here is awake at the moment, on any day and have a rough idea of what is ahead of us but we don't really know for certain. You'll be aware of the saying, "there are only two certainties in life, taxation and dying." It may sound like a rather morbid beginning but I promise the next two points will be more hopeful. It's interesting that the Psalmist wrote along the same lines as in verse 14 "When morning comes let your love satisfy all our needs." People try to remove uncertainty by various means, perhaps through fortune tellers of various descriptions, tea leaves, crystal balls, tarot cards, psychics, horoscopes. In my opinion they are alright for comic relief but not to be relied on. The thing is, nobody knows. I hadn't been long at Somerville House a Uniting Church Presbyterian Girls' School, as Chaplain when the school counsellor asked me to talk to a group of girls who had been using a Ouija board. That is, a game type board where a plastic deal in the middle moves when one's hand is on it and points to certain outcomes. One girl had become convinced that she would die the next day. I had great trouble dissuading them that this was not the case being aware that she could be distracted and trip or be unaware of traffic. Fortunately, she survived the next day and I hope I was successful in persuading them not to dabble in the activity again. We don't know what lies ahead. If we did, we might never leave the house. I have to say I've adopted my mother's practice, unconsciously if not consciously, when planning some event, excursion or travel—"all being well."

HOPING FOR THE BEST

If we don't have hope, then life really loses meaning and we lose incentive. One of the saddest situations which can occur is when someone feels that they are out of options, that life holds nothing further for them. In one of his greatest statements Paul wrote at the end of his words about love to the people in the church at Corinth, "Now abides faith, hope and love but the greatest of these is love." So, he rated hope just behind love as the greatest thing in the world. The psychiatrist Victor Frankl who spent a great deal of the Second World war in concentration camp in Germany tells a very pertinent story in his book "Man's Search for Meaning" One of his fellow inmates had a vivid dream in which he saw their liberation occurring at the end of a certain month. He was convinced that it was some sort of prophecy. Victor Frankl and his other friends tried to convince him not to be so sure, without success. The day came and went without any sign of liberation and in a couple of days, in his debilitated state, he died. It's a literal illustration of the truth that without hope there is no worthwhile life.

NOT WHY BUT HOW

When we face reality, we know that things don't always turn out well, no one can avoid pain, loss, hardship, death at some time, not even those who believe in God and seek to do what God wants. We're not promised this in the Bible, although we might think it is the case until we come up against some distressing loss. People of faith have struggled with this fact for centuries. We see it working out in the Bible. In the early days the ancient Jews linked calamity and prosperity with the degree of their faith and the rightness or otherwise of their actions. The whole book of Job wrestles with the problem of why calamities happen to a righteous man. Jesus himself faced the issue and at one stage asked the people, "What about those 18 people who died when the tower of Siloam fell on them? Do you think they were worse than everyone else in Jerusalem? Not at all. (Luke 13: 4-5) Rabbi Kushner has written a great little book, "Why do bad things happen to good people?"

When we face loss, pain, situations which make us grieve, the question to ask is not why? but how? Not why did this happen to me but how can we handle it. It is possible for people to bring sickness and loss on themselves, such as continuing to take various types of drugs, in spite of the constant warnings of possible harm or someone driving when they know they have had too much alcohol to drink. In more recent years medical science has told us that some conditions such as arthritis and many others could be passed on genetically, people who involve themselves in extreme sports know the risks they take. When some painful situation arises out of the blue affecting either ourselves or a loved one or friend, the question to ask is how can I deal with this. When, for whatever reason a person faces a future disabled in some way there are two huge steps to be taken if one is to deal with it, neither of them is easy. The first is acceptance Paul the apostle struggled with this. He wrote of a "thorn in the flesh"—"a sharp physical pain" of some sort—no one knows just what this was, some have thought epilepsy. He asked for it to be removed but it never was. He had to learn to live with it with the thought that God's strength is made perfect in weakness. Put simply, he had to learn to accept whatever it was. (2 Corinthians 12: 8-9) The next step is adaptation, living with it, perhaps changing how one goes about things. There are many examples of this in news reports of people who have adapted to severe disabilities to live worthwhile lives.

This is where the church at its best comes into its own providing acceptance and support for those who suffer loss of any description. There is a beautiful prayer which fits into this situation—"God grant me the serenity to accept the things I cannot change, the courage to change the things I can and the wisdom to know the difference." Amen.

QUESTIONS

1. Do you sometimes consider the uncertainty of life? What approach to life, in general works for you? If in a group, please share. What is your attitude to the methods for foretelling the future listed in Point 1?

2. Some people seem to be naturally optimistic. How would you rate yourself on a scale to do with optimism with 0 indicating very little and 10 being very optimistic? Do you consider the Christian message inspires hope? What is your hope for the future for a. yourself b. your family c. your nation d. the world?

3. Point 3 outlines the developing process in the Bible towards dealing with suffering and loss. Do you think the outcomes are helpful? Have you had to deal with disability and/or loss yourself or that of a member of your family? If in a group, please share. Is the idea of not asking why in the face of disability or loss but how do I deal with it, helpful?

Isaiah 61:10 "I celebrate and shout because of my Lord God. His saving power and justice are the very clothes I wear."

Wearing Justice

INTRODUCTION

For Isaiah and the other prophets and for Jesus, justice was a prime topic and mission. The prophets spoke of God's justice and called on their people to be just. When Jesus came into the world he continued in this tradition and built on it.

JUSTICE DEFINED

It was easy to dream up the title of this point for it is necessary to consider what we're talking about but it's harder to get at the meaning. Often justice has a hard ring to it as in rough or tough justice. It has been rightly often said that Jesus did support justice but it is tinged with mercy. We often speak of someone getting their just desserts. Justice is often used in connection with the law and punishment for breaking the law. It would be easy to get into a discussion of the penalties for breaking the law in our country, to me thankfully this does not involve capital or corporal punishment but time in prison. Human beings being who they are it is not possible for a society to function without a system of law and punishment. Early in my chaplaincy at Frankston High in Melbourne I met a student, Fiona, who was one of the brightest people I have known. Sadly, she attempted suicide. She believed firmly that anarchy was the system society should follow. In other words, the absence of laws, rules, with people being allowed to do what they want. I couldn't agree with her as human beings are far from being perfect. I feel that all that being said to get our heads around justice in relation to the Christian faith, it is helpful to substitute "fairness" for justice. People need to be treated fairly and in the last point I will make some suggestions as to applications of fairness. Maybe you're thinking but life isn't necessarily fair and this is often the case.

PUTTING ON JUSTICE

I want to look at the expression Isaiah uses, wearing justice like clothes. It's interesting that Paul uses the same expression in his letter to the church at Colossae, in the Good News Bible translation. You are the people of God; he loved you and chose you for his own. So then, you must clothe yourselves with compassion, kindness, humility, gentleness, and patience (Colossians 3:12). There's a saying, "clothes don't make the man (person)" and, of course, that is right, but the meaning here is to consciously put on or adopt these qualities. In other words, this is not something that miraculously happens. Following Jesus is a way of life, the motivation to adopt these attitudes may come about suddenly but it is the start of a process, it is an aim. Being a part of a church provides a constant reminder of what we are about as Christians and provides the opportunity to seek forgiveness for failures and the incentive to continue on the way of Jesus.

FAIRNESS ACROSS THE BOARD

In this final point we'll look at applying fairness across the board. It's a little like the practice that was popular in my earlier schooling to put one's address as such and such a street, suburb, town, country, world, universe. Following are some suggestions for fairness, first of all in one's family, towards ones spouse I think fairness is shown in loyalty, to children seeking to avoid favouring one over the other, in the church even though it's not possible to like everyone being consistent and respectful to each member, in the community getting beyond prejudice, treating people with respect and consideration no matter what race, colour, occupation or position, in the nation to be aware of how people are being treated to seek to oppose discrimination. I'm not seeking to be political here but Australia has a lot to answer for in the treatment of immigrants, to look closely at the fairness or otherwise of how those who break the law are treated and to seek that all have access to education, medical care, welfare. Aboriginal people need to be accepted and brought up to the same level of health and education as every Australian. In the world the challenge is to seek for all people to be free of slavery of any description and to be adequately fed and clothed and housed. We can support the Christmas bowl and all the other agencies such as Amnesty International, Red Cross, Medicine sans Frontiers, United Nations.

This verse from Isaiah is a challenge to check our attitudes and re-adopt fairness. Amen

QUESTIONS

1. Would you say that Australia or your nation stands as an example to the world as a nation which practises widespread justice? Why, or why not? What practices do you favour? What would you like to see changed?
2. Is it possible to ensure that, at least, people in the church practise or support justice for all in society, both your own and the world at large? How?
3. In Point 3 the practise of justice as fair attitudes is outlined for the individual, the family, the community etc. Please check each category, would you extend any of them. If in a group, please share.

Ezekiel 37 :1-14 *particularly* vs 11 "The Lord said, Ezekiel, the people of Israel are like dead bones. They complain that they are dried up and have no hope for the future.

Hope and Life

INTRODUCTION

A large number of the people of Israel had been taken into exile by Babylon when their country had suffered defeat. This was, of course, an horrendous event. The exile took place about 580 BC. Ezekiel who was a priest and a prophet had been taken with them. In his role as a prophet he was God's messenger to the people. Prophets loved using what they saw around them as the basis for their message. Commentators suggest that at some stage Ezekiel had come across an old battle ground where the bones of those who had been killed in the battle were strewn around. He was, of course, aware of the feelings of the people and felt that they were indeed like the dried bones but they could have life and hope.

THE CLOSELY LINKED PAIR

I think we're familiar with the saying "where there's life, there's hope." It's usually used when someone has gone through a rather threatening situation in which they may have lost a good deal of what they depend on but they are still alive. There is obvious truth in the saying. It is also true to say where there is hope there is life. This is what Ezekiel was on about. Where anybody gets to feel that their situation or circumstances are hopeless then they generally lack vitality and may even feel that life is not worth living. In his little book, "Man's Search for Meaning," Victor Frankl, psychiatrist who spent a number of years in concentration camp in Germany during the Second World War writes of a man in the camp who had a very vivid vision of the end of their imprisonment. It was on a specific day. Victor Frankl and others tried to dissuade him from his dependence on this specific day without success. The idea gave him new energy and fresh ability to put up with the horrific conditions. The day came and went but there was no hint of them gaining their freedom. He lost all hope and within a couple of days he died. It's a very stark illustration of the linkage of hope and life.

THE CURRENT SITUATION

The situation in which Ezekiel and his people found themselves was grim. They were in a foreign country forcibly removed from their homes and possibly separated from their families as some of the nation remained in Israel. What about our own situation, nationally, globally, as a church and personally. There is much to shock us globally. It seems difficult for humankind to get beyond racism but just as has been emphasised for us in the view from outer space, we are one planet, earth, and the electronic age and the ease of travel has thrown us together no matter where we were born, what colour we happen to be, or what traditional religion we espouse. That said there is much that is disturbing in the world, wars, famines, people without a country, poverty, oppression, threats to the environment. The church is struggling in many places. Overall, Christianity is still the most numerous religion. Within our own situation we are surviving but there are signs of hope.

EZEKIEL'S INPUT

We'll look at Ezekiel's suggestions to raise hope and bring life. His instructions were to prophesy to the bones. To preach to them, if you like, which was what prophets did. They looked at the situation they found themselves in and through their understanding of what God wanted spoke to the situation. In effect this is what preaching is all about, if the interpretation of a passage of scripture is faithful and insightful it can make a difference and as we meet here at this time there's a lot of preaching going on around the world. Let's not forget that the best sermons are in the attitudes we adopt from day to day. Ezekiel also called on the wind to blow over the bones. In Hebrew the language in which the Old Testament was written the same word is used for wind, breath and spirit. Hence on the Day of Pentecost there was the sound of a rushing mighty wind. We may not have anything approaching what was described on the day of Pentecost but we meet together for mutual support, we ponder the Scriptures particularly the Gospels, we sing together, we pray together. It's a chance to be recharged and hopefully we become more open to the needs and concerns of people no matter what nation, colour, culture or religion and in intercession reach across the world. At the end of Jesus's brief three-year ministry as he followed out his espousal of nonviolence, love and oneness with suffering and went to a cross his disciples were in despair but they came through that with him as expressed in the great Sidney Carter hymn, "I danced in the morning," "they cut me down but I leap up high." The impact of this came home to me years ago when we attended a performance of the Rock musical, "Godspell." It was put on by the young people at St. Andrews church in Frankston, Melbourne and was very well done. After the crucifixion scene, some of the disciples carried the dead Jesus, at shoulder height from the church to a dirge like refrain. There was the impression it was the end of the musical but in a complete change of mood, the participants came screaming back into the church. The music changed to a lively, loud rock piece. The atmosphere was electric, Jesus had risen.

QUESTIONS

You'll notice there is only one question but it is three pronged and rather massive.

1. If you are in a group, at each part please share your thoughts. If by yourself, please consider responses and perhaps write

Hope and Life

them down. Where have you found hope in a personal situation of stress and/or loss and what signs of hope do you see in the world's crises of conflict, prejudice, lack of life's essentials, and the effects of climate change and what signs of hope have you seen or hope to see for the spreading of the church's message?

> **Matthew 2: 14** "That night Joseph got up and took his wife and the child to Egypt."

Saving the Message

INTRODUCTION

The inclusion of the coming of the Magi or "wise men" in the story of the birth of Jesus widens its impact. One of the effects of their seeking to see Jesus was to warn Herod of a possible future king to threaten his rule. His horrific reaction, the killing of all baby boys two years old and under, led to Joseph going with Mary and baby Jesus to Egypt. It's interesting to see the parallels with the Pharoah of Egypt's efforts to kill baby boys to reduce the future population of Jews in Egypt at the time of Moses.

THE FLIGHT TO EGYPT AND THE COPTIC CHURCH

There is a metal relief of the flight to Egypt on one of the walls in the Coptic quarter of Cairo, probably on St. Sargius Church which is also on the booklet we picked up in the church when we went there as part of a trip to Egypt a few years ago. Under the title is the statement, "the oldest church in Egypt." Apparently, there was a fairly large Jewish community in Egypt at that time and Mary and Joseph would have sought refuge with them. In the booklet I've already mentioned it is stated that it was in this church or building that "the Holy Family" lived during their stay in Egypt.

It would not have been an easy journey for Joseph and Mary, we worked out that it would have been at least 500 kms with Mary on the back of a donkey and Joseph leading the way.

I've used the word Coptic a few times already in this Sermon. Coptic is the term used for the ancient Egyptian language which has been mostly superseded but is still the language used in the rituals of the Coptic Church. It is one of the orthodox churches and came about when St. Mark went to Alexandria in 61 AD and spoke about Jesus. Apparently by the end of the 4th century Christianity had become the official religion of Egypt. The building of churches in different parts of the country began early in the 5th century. The Coptic Church had a large influence on the shaping of Christian creeds particularly through its bishop Athanasius. This changed at the beginning of the 8th century when Islam conquered Egypt. There are approx. 80 million Muslim people in Egypt and it is the dominant religion with some 90% of the population. There are 9 million Christians and I have to say I was surprised by the number.

SAVING THE MESSAGE

Many times I have thought that Joseph is one of the most neglected people in the story of Jesus and the development of his message. In a very few words in our text we have a prime example, "That night Joseph got up and took his wife and the child to Egypt." If he hadn't Jesus would have been killed so he did indeed save the message. We don't know how long they stayed in Egypt but some of the up- bringing of Jesus would have occurred there. They eventually moved back to Galilee and settled in Nazareth and Jesus would have been schooled in the Jewish faith. There is a large gap in our knowledge about the life of Jesus from the birth stories to his journey to Jerusalem with Mary and Joseph when he was about 12 and another from then until he started his ministry at age 30. It is understood that at some stage in that second gap Joseph died but Jesus would have worked with him in the carpenter's shop and as the oldest taken over from him when he died. All this time through his association with his parents and his link with the synagogue and the local Rabbi the message was being shaped, but remember it was Joseph who took Mary and Jesus to safety.

Saving the Message

OUR MESSAGE IS JESUS

In the church my wife Mary and I started attending when we moved to Ipswich, then called Trinity there was a banner hanging on the pulpit. The banner said and depicted, "Jesus, our Message" One would be hard put to find a truer statement. Amidst the multiplicity of denominations to which the church has become subject and the different approaches to ritual in services and the varieties in church organisation and the disastrous misunderstandings of what Jesus was on about as, for example, the inquisition and the crusades, stands these words, "Jesus our message." When anyone espouses the particular belief of following Jesus or Christianity it doesn't matter what that person says about the belief if his or her life isn't in sync. In the case of Jesus his attitudes and actions bore out his teaching. I'm afraid that isn't always possible for the rest of us, which is why we pray regularly to "forgive us our sins as we forgive those who sin against us" It's life shaping stuff. At the start of the Lord's Prayer we say, "your kingdom come, your will be done on earth." The second clause fills out the meaning of the first. We're praying that people might be ready to do what God wants. What does God want, to live as close as possible to the life, attitudes and teaching of Jesus. I want to suggest there's no better overall resolution at any stage of our lives and with it goes a desire for the peace, goodwill, compassion and concern Jesus came to bring. Amen

QUESTIONS

1. The facts about the spread of Christianity to Egypt set out in the first point make amazing reading. Christianity has indeed gone into all the world. What are your thoughts about its continued spread? Do you see possibilities of working with other religions such as Buddhism, Hinduism, Islam, Judaism and others for the wellbeing of humankind?

2. Any thoughts about the glaring neglect of Joseph in the Gospels and Christian history.

3. Someone at one time said to another person advocating the Christian faith something like, I cannot hear what you're saying because what you are is too loud in my ears, a hugely derogatory statement. Is there a good way to speak about the worthwhileness of seeking to follow Jesus? If so, what is it?

Matthew 4:8–10 "The devil took Jesus up a very high mountain and showed him all the kingdoms on earth and their power. The devil said to him. "I will give all this to you, if you will bow down and worship me." Jesus answered, "Go away, Satan! The Scriptures say; Worship the Lord your God and serve only him."

A Pivotal Decision

INTRODUCTION

The incident described in this passage from Matthew occurred immediately following the baptism of Jesus by John when Jesus felt affirmed by God. The urge was to get away by himself. Matthew suggested Jesus was 40 days in a desert place which seems to parallel the 40 years the Children of Israel spent in the wilderness. I think Jesus used this time to sort out how he would go about his ministry and that what is described was going on in his mind which he must have later spoken about to his disciples as it is included in the Gospels.

THE CHOICE JESUS MADE

The final image in this sorting out process, having rejected the first two, using his powers to feed people, and acts of magic like surviving jumping off the temple, was to rule over the various kingdoms of the world, using evil, possibly violent ways with the aim of control. He rejected that possibility out of hand as shown in the way he went about his ministry seeking to influence people by what he said and did and the attitudes he had. This was a massive choice Jesus made. Jewish people have had an often-disastrous history, partly due to the location of their country with countries from the East such as Babylon and Assyria marching through their land and the Egyptians from the South threatening them. Jewish people have moved throughout the world and most recently were

A Pivotal Decision

subjected to the horrors of the holocaust. The people of the days of Jesus looked to the coming of the Messiah, the Christ, God's chosen one, someone like David, their king of old who would bring about another heyday of the Jews. They hoped for a messiah who would overthrow their current oppressor, the Romans. When Jesus began moving around the country teaching in a way that was fresh and challenging and healing people, they began to feel he was special and hope above hope, maybe he was such a Messiah. The way they felt was shown in the welcome they gave him as he rode into Jerusalem on a donkey. He would only have needed to say the word and they would have rallied to him and taken on the Romans. Jesus, however, had made his choice, 3 years before in the desert, and he wasn't about to use violence to establish a kingdom, his was a kingdom of love, compassion and concern.

BEING REALLY GREAT MEANS TO SERVE

When Jesus on one occasion was asked by the mother of John and James if they could have a privileged position in Jesus's kingdom much to the disgust of the other disciples, he finished up by saying, in effect, that true greatness comes through service. Many human beings have a desire for position and privilege and really this is the case throughout society. Really it doesn't matter what organisation we're thinking about or form of government or the church. Always there is a need for leadership and some are more naturally leaders than others and sometimes people feel a responsibility to offer to lead even though it's not their natural inclination. I don't think there is anything wrong with ambition, with a desire to make the most of oneself but the real test of the quality of leadership is the extent of one's readiness to serve. Accolades may come but if anyone is following these words of Jesus, they are not sought after. Jesus followed out his desire to serve and his dedication to non-violence to a cross.

THE PIVOTAL DECISION

Jesus's dismissal of the idea to use violent means to influence communities was with the words, "Worship the Lord your God and serve only him." What or who we worship makes up what is at the centre of our lives and motivates us. John said a great deal when he wrote, "God is love." To worship God is to put love at the centre of life and to have love as our main motivation, the main driving force of our actions and decisions. Fortunately, I believe, we have had spelt out for us in the life, teaching and attitudes of Jesus, this sort of love, it's to do with compassion, concern, a getting rid of hatred and prejudice, a seeking of the well-being of people around us. I believe it is important to our progress in life to take time to check how we're going, to seek forgiveness, may be to reconcile differences. In my early days in Sunday School once a year Decision Day was held. We were challenged to make a Decision to follow Jesus and we signed a Card indicating our decision. I didn't really realise at the time the repercussions of that decision but looking back I'm happy I made it. In the light of all the studies which followed and theological studies and discussions, it was and is a simple decision and an illustration of the fact that often the Christian life is made way too complex and controversial. These words of Jesus challenge us to ask what is the centre of our lives.

QUESTIONS

1. The Gospel writers obviously accepted the existence of "the devil" who is credited with the "temptations" of Jesus in a desert region. Do you personally believe in the existence of the devil? Why? or Why not?

2. Jesus chose a way of complete nonviolence in the pursuit of his mission. Historically he has been followed, most prominently by Mahatma Gandhi and Martin Luther King. What is your attitude towards nonviolence? Would you or maybe,

A Pivotal Decision

have you taken up arms to defend your country? Was that, or would it be, a difficult decision?

3. Following the way of Jesus, as he pointed out, involves being ready to serve. What form/s of service have you chosen or would you choose?

4. The early disciples commenced their service by responding to a challenge from Jesus, "follow me." Even slight attention to books of theology or general Christian literature, suggest following the way of Jesus is rather complex. How have you found it?

Matthew 5:16 "Make your light shine, so that others will see the good you do and will praise your father in heaven."

Jesus bids us Shine

INTRODUCTION

Years and years ago we occasionally sang a chorus which went," Jesus bids us shine with a clear, pure light, like a little candle burning in the night, in this world is darkness so we must shine, you in your small corner, I in mine. I'll refer back to this later in the sermon. These words of Jesus gave rise to a number of choruses another being "Jesus wants me for a sunbeam" which indicates how much they have caught people's imaginations.

THE MAJOR SOURCE OF LIGHT

I think it's almost automatic when one reads the words Jesus spoke to his disciples, "You are the light of the world" to think of the words he spoke in a different context recorded in John's gospel, "I am the light of the world." It goes along with a series of statements in the same format, such as "I am the water of life," "I am the vine." So when Jesus said to his first disciples as he says to us across the centuries, if we have indicated a readiness to follow him, "You are the light of the world," he was issuing a challenge to follow his tradition, to follow his way. As we read the gospels that way is spelt out in the life and attitudes of Jesus. He obviously enjoyed life and was well aware of what was going on around him. He loved people and did not discriminate unlike many of his contemporaries. He accepted women, he was prepared to associate with those who were regarded as outcasts such as tax collectors and lepers He associated with those of other nations such as Samaritans and Romans. He showed particular concern and compassion for those in need, the poor, the sick, and the oppressed. He was not impressed with the self-righteous perhaps we could say, the over religious. He was nonviolent in his approach to people and life. He spoke of a need to be forgiving and the need to shun revenge. In the prayer which has become known as his particular prayer he advocated confessing our short comings but not to expect forgiveness if we don't forgive others, "forgive us our sins as we forgive those who sin against us."

A LITTLE LIGHT COUNTS

In this point I'm really going back to the chorus I quoted in the introduction which finishes, "You in your small corner and I in mine." Most of us don't cause a blaze by the way we live. We're not asked to. We follow our aptitudes and interests and circumstances into certain areas of work, we may meet a certain special person and establish a family. The rest of what I want to say in this point will be through a couple of stories. In the last few years of my time as Chaplain of Somerville House, a Uniting and Presbyterian Church girl's school of about a 1000, the Principal at the time Dr Murray Evans decided to introduce a very significant conclusion to the Valedictory Service for the Year 12 students. They were all given candles and at the end of the service, the lights in the Assembly Hall were switched off. Someone lit the candle of the girl nearest the aisle and then progressively the candles of each girl were lit. This meant that from the stage gradually the face of each one was lit up and became clear. After I had been there 5 years I had come to know them all, and one couldn't help but wonder what contribution they would make to the world. They then processed out and there was a supper provided and sadly, for me, most of them went down to Schoolies. All the time, the piece of music, "Gabriel's Oboe" was played from the music for the movie, "The Mission."

The second story is an account I read years ago of a huge rally which was held. I'd like to think it was World Council of churches or United nations. It was held in a large enclosed stadium. As the people had come into the stadium they were each given a box of matches. At one point in the rally the lights were turned off and the people asked to strike their matches. The stadium lit up amazingly but because of the individual light from each person. An illustration of the change that is possible when people of good will of various religions or no religion seek to live for the benefit of human kind.

IT'S ACTIONS WHICH COUNT

The light which Jesus spoke about shows itself mainly in the good or good things one does as set out in this verse. In other words in actions. How we treat people, how we act towards them, how we serve or help them is the clearest way to show our love or concern. Eliza Doolittle in "My Fair Lady" was emphatic in challenging the men in her life to not just speak of love but rather show her. The verse we're focussing on is not the only part of teaching of Jesus which stresses that it is not how much we profess faith or not how long we spend in worship or prayer which is most pleasing to God but rather in what we do to express our concern for people no matter what their creed or colour. I think that is a good interpretation of the last words of this verse, "and will praise your father in heaven" after seeing the good things we do. John wrote with great insight, "God is love." I can't think of any better way to finish than the way I started that Jesus does indeed bid us shine, you in your small corner and I in mine.

QUESTIONS

1. Christianity has spread tremendously across the world and has become the most numerous religion. What positive effects do you consider Christianity has had in the places to which it has spread?

Jesus bids us Shine

2. Do you consider that following Jesus has lit up your life, so to speak? In what way?

3. Can you think of a time/s when words seemed inadequate, perhaps just a presence was? Can you think of positive actions people took which meant a lot to you or that you took towards others?

Matthew 14:20 "After everyone had eaten all they wanted, Jesus' disciples picked up 12 baskets of left overs."

More than Sufficient

INTRODUCTION

Some years ago Mary and I visited Israel. I say this in spite of our oldest son saying that he read that someone in America whose church was about to call a minister said that he didn't want anyone who would keep on saying, "When I visited Israel" or who said, "there are 4 words in Greek for love." On one day of our visit we hired a taxi for the same price we would have paid for a tour when we missed out on a booking. He drove us where we wanted to go for a day. We wanted to go to the Sea of Galilee because so much in the life of Jesus happened there. We had lunch at a restaurant on a hill overlooking the Sea. The taxi driver said that the feeding of the 5000 took place on a grassy hill which sloped to the sea. It was certainly believable.

THE FEEDING

All of the gospels mention this incident and in this point I just want to draw attention to some of the things mentioned. For a start it should be pointed out that you ladies and the children present need to take umbrage because you don't get included in the count. There were 5000 men present which probably means there were about 10,000 present if women and children had been included. Those calculations are understandable given that this was in about 31 AD and it was a patriarchal society. We could talk about the situation today but there's too much else to cover.

John includes the story of Andrew finding a boy who was ready to share his lunch. There are a number of commentators who suggest that what could have happened on that day was that when a number of people saw the boy offer his lunch, they felt they should offer to share what they had. It's certainly an interesting thought. As people have thought about this incident and their number is enormous when you consider that it's been going on for nearly 2000 years, some have been rather mystified about the apparent contradiction in Jesus's attitude. In his time in a desert region at the start of his ministry, known as his temptations, when I think he sorted out how to go about his ministry, one of the thoughts he had was to turn stones into bread when he felt hungry. He rejected that idea. One point is that at that time in the desert it was his own hunger that he was dealing with whereas here it was a whole crowd of people. There's another thought that what Jesus did, paralleled the time when the Jews were being led by Moses across the so-called wilderness. They complained bitterly about their hunger. One of the sources of food was manna which was collected in the morning. At first it was thought the manna was an excretion of the tamarisk but a later thought is that it was the excretion of two types of scale insects. All of these things mentioned occur naturally in the Sinai.

MORE THAN SUFFICIENT

I believe there's another parallel in that there are 12 baskets of left overs, the same number as the 12 tribes of Israel. I believe, however, the real point of there being more than enough is just that. The provision was more than adequate. Another important point is that Jesus was concerned about the physical needs of the people. We'll think of other needs in the final point. It's very difficult to think of less concrete needs if one is hungry. The tummy rumbles of 10,000 people would have drowned out anything else. There are people starving throughout the world, although there are a number of organisations who offer help. In some parts of the world children may grow up without ever knowing what it means not to be hungry. There are of course reasons for this. They range from drought to a poor distribution of a nation's resources, to absolute greed. When I googled this subject I found a quote from the World Trade Organisation, "if the total calories from all the food produced on earth was divided among all the people on earth there would be 2750 calories per person per day." The recommended daily minimum per person is 2,100 calories per day. This is a very complex issue, amongst other factors including politics but the point I want to make which I believe flows naturally from this incident in the life of Jesus is that there is more than sufficient food in the world for all people.

THE BREAD OF LIFE

It is after John's account of the feeding of the 5000 that in speaking to the people Jesus refers to himself as "the bread of life." The extended passage is John 6:1–56. This certainly is John's account of what we have come to know as the Lord's Supper, known by different names amongst the churches it is still the central service of the Christian church. It is a linking of followers of Jesus with the person we meet in the gospels, reminding us of the attitudes and concerns he had, the attitudes and concerns of one who was also a human being. Bread is part of the staple diet of many peoples around the world. I believe that if we are to get the most from life and give the most to it, we need to follow Jesus, to know his words and attitudes, and seek to live them out. The church which Paul called "the body of Christ" is here to constantly draw our attention to Jesus, to seek to carry out his concerns and to provide companionship and support along the way. Amen

QUESTIONS

1. There are a number of interpretations of the account of the feeding of the 5000+ in the first point. What is your reaction to them?

2. Jesus was obviously very concerned about the privations of a number of people of his day and therefore his concern has passed on to those who seek to follow his way. Has your church been active to help? If so. How? Have you acted to help?

3. What does the Sacrament of Holy Communion, whatever its name in your denomination, mean to you? If in a group share your thoughts about your participation.

Matthew 23:10 "None of you should be called the leader"

Individual Worth

INTRODUCTION

One of the key sayings of Jesus is recorded in John 10:10 "I came so everyone would have life, and have it in its fullest." It leads very well into this verse.

ALL HAVE WORTH

One way of looking at this verse is to suggest that if no one is to be called leader then everyone has the potential to be leader and everyone is of equal worth. A prime part of Human Relationships Education is the concept of self-esteem. In other words, one of the aims is to help individuals to realise their own worth and so to recognise that they have a contribution to make to any organisation or activity in which they wish to participate. When Jesus was asked on one occasion which was the greatest commandment, the second one which he quoted from the Jewish Scriptures and had been around even then for centuries was to "love people as much as you love yourself." Those words confirm the place of self-esteem in acceptance of ourselves and the recognition that we have our place in the world, wherever that may be. This means we have a standard by which to govern how we treat others. Jesus, in the passage we're considering was scathing in his criticism of many of the Jewish religious leaders in their flaunting of many of the trappings of their leadership such as having texts of scripture strapped on their foreheads and huge tassels on their robes. Perhaps Jesus

Individual Worth

would have been more accepting of these practices if he didn't feel that they were putting themselves above others. I believe it is in reaction to their elevating of themselves which led Jesus to say such things as "none of you should be called teacher or leader." Jesus very often made his point by use of exaggeration. Jesus spoke of "humbling oneself." I feel that only works if one is in danger of getting a big head because of some achievement or other. For the average person to put themselves down is to withdraw themselves from getting the most out of life and giving the most to it.

THE PRIESTHOOD OF ALL BELIEVERS

Jesus seemed to be very much against the use of titles in religion, rabbi and so on. The function of a priest was and still is to be a mediator between people and God. If we extend the title to minister, or pastor I guess the role is to be a type of guide in the affairs of church and faith. In the first letter of Peter 2:5 the writer states to the people in the church he was writing to, "You are also a group of holy priests." From words such as those came the term, "the priesthood of all believers." In others words everyone has direct access to God everyone is their own minister or whatever term is used for the position in the various churches. It's a hugely democratic statement which has had varying degrees of observance throughout the History of the churches. To cut down on ambition purely for status amongst the clergy in some churches there is no increase in stipend or wages no matter what position the particular clergy person holds.

BUT—NOT ANARCHY

So where does that leave people like myself, priests, ministers, pastors and all the other titles.? Does the idea of the Priesthood of all believers leave us without a particular role? Can a church survive, let alone thrive without the appointment of some representative of the clergy. The answer, of course, is that it has happened on many

Individual Worth

occasions but I think that there is a greater chance of advancement when there is someone with training to take overall responsibility. I feel it's a no-brainer to believe that any organisation can survive without someone taking specific responsibility. I think there's some point in telling my own story in regard to ministry. I grew up in Graceville Methodist Church and thanks to my parents was heavily involved in the church and enjoyed it. As the end of High School approached, I would sit in church listening to sermons wondering what I was going to do with myself beyond High School. I didn't have a clue. One thing I was certain about was that I didn't want to do anything which took me away from what I was familiar with in regard to family and church. I certainly didn't show signs of leadership aptitude although a pro- prefect in Year 12. When a friend of mine who hadn't got as good a pass in Senior decided to do Medicine I felt if he could do it so could I and I had the idea of becoming a Medical Missionary. I failed Year 1 of Med. miserably as did my friend. He repeated and eventually became a successful GP. I knew I couldn't repeat. It just wasn't me and as I look back, I wonder how I ever thought it could be. As I cast around for the next step, it seemed that it was in training for the ministry given my large involvement in the church. I read a little later when someone was describing finding direction in life that there is one course which could be described as "open and shut doors" which was the door of one course of action slamming in one's face but then another door opening. It's not the only time in my life in which circumstances have guided a decision. It's how one reacts to circumstances which counts. So began 8 years of training. The boy who sat in church not wanting to move out of the comfort zone finished up in Oakey, Fiji, San Diego, Denver, Melbourne. I have told that story to illustrate how someone ends up being a minister. I can't speak for all the churches but there are many interviews and tests before beginning training. Depending on one's background there will be courses of study, common elements would be Bible, church history, theology, preaching, leading worship. There will be other focuses, for me, Psychology of Religion and Pastoral Care. Someone told me at one time that in spite of training to be a teacher one learns to teach by

Individual Worth

teaching and one learns to be a minister by ministering. I believe the key to worthwhile service in the church and beyond is in the words of Jesus, "Whoever is the greatest should be the servant of others." To minister means to serve so that whatever one's role in the church might be the challenge is to serve. Each person has a role in ministry which is what is meant by "priesthood of all believers." As followers of Jesus, we find ongoing incentive and support for ministry within the church but the extension is into the community as we go about our daily lives. Amen.

QUESTIONS

1. Many young people, very often, tend to "put themselves down" rather than recognise their self-worth. How would you go about seeking to bolster their self-esteem?

2. On a scale of 1–10 with 10 being maximum, how would you rate your own self esteem?

3. Does the, "priesthood of all believers" make sense to you? Can you see or have you seen this system at work?

4. What's your story in regard to where you are and what you're doing in life? If you're considering this by yourself, perhaps you'd like to write it down. If in a group, perhaps you'd like to share.

Matthew 25: 31–46 Parable of Sheep and Goats

Jesus and People

INTRODUCTION

The heading of the second point of this sermon is, "The Heart of the Gospel" and I believe this parable does do just that, put forward the very heart of the Gospel or Good News of Jesus. When referring to it I like to point out two views which have mostly changed. In Jesus's day, obviously shepherds and others favoured sheep over goats, so that in the example of the last judgment, those who were acceptable were like sheep those who were unacceptable were like goats, and goats over the centuries have proven their worth. Also those who were unacceptable were put on the left. Left handedness then was thought to be unnatural and this thought has taken a long time to be overcome.

THE KINGDOM OF GOD

All the parables in the Gospels are about the Kingdom of God. They all start with, "The kingdom of God is like . . . " So it was a very important part of the teaching of Jesus but I believe it has been misunderstood many times throughout history. Biblical scholars suggest that a better word than Kingdom is "reign," so the "the reign of God" rather than the Kingdom of God which takes away some of the possibility of associating certain "kingdoms," that is territories as being God's kingdom. The meaning for Jesus is shown in what has become known as "the Lord's prayer." "Your kingdom come and the next phrase spells it out, "your will be done on earth as in heaven." In other words, the Kingdom is made up of those seeking to do what God wants, and that is spelt out in the life and attitudes of Jesus. Towards the start of the ministry of Jesus there is an account, often known as the "temptations of Jesus" which took place in a wilderness area. I think they are best thought of as Jesus working out how he would go about his ministry. In the last one where he seems to envision territories of earth and the possibility of ruling them, Jesus turns his back on the idea. He would work by loving people, having compassion for them, and with positive ideas and attitudes. Ministers favour political parties in their preaching to their peril, but I'm going to venture a political type opinion. In spite of my father being a bank manger when he retired, our two older sons being in the higher realms of finance and having two grandsons in financial advice, finances and the economy have never been one of my strong points. However I have decided that "capitalism" is the most likely economic system to work. However, I believe that anyone who is seriously seeking to follow the way of Jesus couldn't read this passage and others like it and ignore or neglect the needs of the underprivileged, the down trodden or impoverished.

THE HEART OF THE GOSPEL

So to "The Heart of the Gospel." I want to lead into this with part of my personal faith journey. I don't consider I went through adolescence till my forties some would say I've never got beyond it. I grew up in a strongly Methodist church and home where there was an emphasis on "Christian assurance," the apostle Paul's emphasis, strongly adopted by John Wesley, the Anglican minister whose experience at a church in Aldersgate St. in London, revolutionised faith in England at the time. Throughout my adolescence, I searched for that experience, services, reading, discussion groups, camps, study,- that is, the ongoing sense of acceptance, so much so that as I looked back I felt I had bypassed what the psychiatrist, Eric Ericson suggested was the main task of adolescence, realising one's identity, one's uniqueness. Ericson set out 8 tasks for human beings from infancy through old age. In adolescence he suggests it is, "Identity vs. role confusion." It was during my second major bout of study in America that I came to a point of realising, that's not for me, what was for me was the simple but thorough commitment to following Jesus, the feelings come and go. In this passage I think, following Jesus leads us to seeing the unfailing worth of every individual, no matter what their circumstances and we're to treat them as if they were Jesus himself. Bringing this parable down to earth, I believe Jesus made it very plain, an acceptable life for anyone is measured not by what they believe, what they call their faith, what church denomination they are a part of, what their religious experience is, but how they treat the rest of human kind and I think he would add, how they treat everything else that has life and the earth.

JESUS AND PEOPLE

Jesus sets out the basic needs of people in the parable, for food, drink, company, that is, relationships, clothing, medical care, and care in prison if one transgresses the law. The point of my comment that the test of worthwhile living is one's attitude to people particularly those with obvious needs becomes very plain and also the place of philanthropy, compassion and concern and the church over the centuries has led in many of these areas. I don't think I need to drive the point home any further but over the years I've wondered about his mention of prison. At first I thought he was considering those persecuted for their beliefs, but I'm convinced it was much wider than that. I realise the church has made constant efforts in this direction through chaplaincy and so on but it's an area where society has a lot of work to do. We speak of justice, a Mennonite professor I read recently spoke of "restorative justice" as against "retributive justice." I think very often justice is seen as retribution but what is needed is work towards change. Human beings are very tribal, think of the multiplicity of Christian denominations. Once established it is extremely difficult to return to unity, but more to the point, race, nation and class. The hymn, written by

Sydney Carter," When I needed a neighbour" based, in part on this parable, has the chorus suggested by the teaching and attitudes of Jesus, "And the creed and the colour and the name won't matter."

I want to conclude by stressing again what I believe Jesus made clear in this parable that each individual is unique and important and as he also made clear in other parts of his ministry that sense of concern extends to all that has life and the earth. Paul the apostle in an inspired moment called the church, the body of Christ. Our task and it is a huge one is to represent him and continue to seek to recommend his teaching and attitudes. Amen

QUESTIONS

1. The Kingdom of God or Of Heaven was the major focus of Jesus's mission. How familiar are you with what the kingdom involves? How often have you been aware of it being the basis of a sermon? How could you and the church spread the kingdom?

2. What, if anything brought you to becoming a follower of Jesus or a devout church member, a Christian. Do you think that process has helped your personal development?

3. Do you think this concept which Jesus had of identifying with people, "when did we see you hungry etc." helps you to accept the importance of the individual?

4. Are you surprised Jesus seems to have identified with those in prison? What is your attitude to capital punishment? How could the prison service be improved?

Mark 1:4 "John the Baptist showed up in the desert and told everyone, "Turn back to God (repent) and be baptised. Then you will be forgiven."

New Beginnings

INTRODUCTION

John who became known as the Baptist was an interesting figure. He lived in the desert surviving on locusts and wild honey. Incidentally, it's interesting that a number of people strongly recommend the place of insects in diet. He definitely did not believe in comfort wearing clothes made from camel hair. He was imprisoned by Herod as a result of his strong criticism of Herod's personal life and was executed in prison. He began preaching when Jesus was about 30, called for people to repent and practised baptism, so that he baptised Jesus.

REPENTANCE

John challenged his listeners to repent. I prefer the older translations of the word John used, that is, repent, although there's nothing wrong with the translation in the "The Bible for Today," "Turn back to God." I think the word, "repent" is more expressive. It means to do an about turn, to change direction. The about turns in someone's life which are the most obvious are those which occur when for whatever reason someone who has really lost their way perhaps through drugs, or criminal activity of some sort, has an awakening and begins to live a positive and worthwhile life and it has happened and happens. I grew up in an evangelical home and church so many times heard appeals from the pulpit to give my life to Jesus. I responded and have to say, that the appeals I heard were rather compelling so that many times I had to resist responding again. Thanks to my home and church life I didn't go off the deep end but the response which meant the most was in my head when I decided that I simply wanted to follow Jesus and that's been a way of life. Having said all that, I think, it's good at times to go back to basics as it were and check how we're going, have we perhaps gone off on a tangent in the way we're living or misunderstood the simple, down to earth message which Jesus advocated.

BAPTISM

John challenged the people to whom he spoke to be baptised. This was to be the definite sign that they were sincere in their desire to change. This point could be a whole other sermon and books have been written on the topic and it is a matter of debate between churches. The debate comes about mainly because in the early church once families started to come into the church baptism of infants commenced. There can obviously be no debate about the fact that when John baptised in the Jordan, baptism was by immersion, the person was put under the water by John and, of course, this is the form of baptism practised in Baptist, Church of Christ and Pentecostal churches. In the Uniting Church if someone makes the request, we must be ready to make arrangements for such a baptism to take place, or possibly by pouring when water is poured over the person, or sprinkling which is the form of baptism mostly practiced. In churches which practise infant baptism when a person baptised as an infant reaches the age of 12 or beyond by their own decision, they may wish to confirm the decision of their parents on their behalf and decide to become church members. Baptism is a time-honoured symbolic practice of cleansing, setting apart, commitment.

NEW BEGINNINGS

This point of the sermon really takes off from John the Baptist's words, "Then you will be forgiven." In those words, implying that people have indicated a readiness to change direction and that they have been missing the mark somewhat. It is a good practice as we seek to follow the way of Jesus to at times consider our progress along that way. I can't think of a better way to examine how we're going in the loving department than going through Paul's definition of love in first Corinthians 13 which I'm about to do. It's good to remember that some of us have less trouble following out some of Paul's suggestions than others might, and that where we are in the age stakes could have a bearing (grumpy old man Syndrome eg) Dare I suggest as I read these, we focus specifically on ourselves, "Love is kind and patient, never jealous, boastful, proud or rude. Love isn't selfish or quick tempered. It doesn't keep a record of wrongs that others do. Love rejoices in the truth but not in evil. Love is always supportive, loyal, hopeful, and trusting. Love never fails." It would be surprising in deed, if we had not slipped up somewhere in that searching list. If we're sorry then the promise is that we can be forgiven and if there is some glaring mistreatment of a particular person or people, they may forgive us if we ask. The main point of this challenge of John the Baptist is that change is an option. John Powell, priest and psychiatrist wrote the telling words, "My attitude has changed therefore everything's changed. That's what it means to follow Jesus. Amen

QUESTIONS

1. Repentance means a complete change of direction, an "about turn." Does this describe your entry to the Christian life? If not, how would you describe your course in life to this point?
2. What form of baptism, if any, have you had? Are you content with the experience of baptism you have had? Why or why not?

3. Paul's definition of love sets out the sort of love we are commanded by Jesus to have in the commandments he said were the most important and his new commandment to his followers to "love one another." Paul's definition is indeed thorough. How do you measure up? Is it too demanding?

Mark 1:17 "Jesus said to them, "Come with me (follow me") I'll teach you how to bring in people instead of fish."

Following the Leader, Jesus

INTRODUCTION

A prominent church leader in America once said when the church he attended was about to get a new minister that he hoped it would be someone who wasn't too enthusiastic about the 4 Greek words for love in the New Testament or who had been to Israel and felt he had to make constant mention. The reason for all that is that Mary, my wife, and I have had a trip to Israel and I want to mention something about it. One of the things I most wanted to do was to walk along the shore of the Sea of Galilee and managed to do it. A lot of incidents in the life of Jesus seemed to happen on or around the sea and it seemed to me to earth him, so to speak. Jesus met the men who were to be his first disciples by the sea. Some translations including "Bible for Today" have the words, "Come with me." Older translations have "Follow me" which I prefer, hence our theme.

FOLLOWING JESUS IN OPENNESS TO ALL PEOPLES

As I said at the beginning of the service I'm wanting to concentrate on following Jesus into his relating to other peoples. We've got some great examples throughout the Gospels. There is the story of Jesus meeting a Samaritan woman at a well as he and his disciples passed through Samaria. This was amazing for two reasons: the first, Jewish men didn't speak to women outside the home even when the woman was his own wife. We need to follow Jesus into consideration of the place of women. Even in our own society where there is concern about women 's rights, there is a long way to go to achieve equal pay for women performing the same jobs as men. Also, women are not equally represented in government and executive roles in business. Of course, there are places across the world such as the Middle East where women are nothing less than repressed. I was reading recently of a woman in Pakistan who in spite of vehement opposition from her father educated herself and went on to establish schools where children could be educated. The second amazing part of the story is that Jesus was meeting a Samaritan citizen. Jews and Samaritans did not usually associate with one another. We need to follow Jesus into acceptance of people of all races and cultures. It is great that we have people from a number of other races in our congregation and, of course, far more are represented in wider society. Prejudice should not be tolerated in ourselves or in society. I also think that it is almost inconceivable that we are needing a referendum to include aboriginal people in the Australian constitution.

FOLLOWING JESUS INTO CONCERN FOR THE NEEDY AND THE OPPRESSED

We need to follow Jesus into concern for those who are needy or oppressed. There are a number of incidents illustrating this in the Gospels. This was a major part of his mission to the world as shown in Luke's gospel as Jesus spoke in the synagogue at Nazareth and quoted from the prophet Isaiah, "The Lord's spirit has come to me, because he has chosen me to tell the good news to the poor, to announce freedom for prisoners, to give sight to the blind." He went on to claim these words for his own. During his ministry he healed lepers, the blind, the paralysed, and championed the poor. The church through the centuries, at its best times has followed Jesus into these areas of concern, and this is still the case with Blue Care, Anglicare and St. Vincent de Paul as examples. The challenge to us as individuals is to reach out to those in need as we have opportunity. I believe that this is one of the strengths of the church to support those going through times of sickness and loss particularly within the congregation.

BRINGING IN PEOPLE

The rest of the verse speaks of Jesus training the men he invited to be with him to bring in people instead of fish. Jesus loved using the setting he found himself in to illustrate his message or purpose, here, the obvious message was fishing. I have to say the image of net fishing for bringing people in is not as stark as fishing with a hook. When I was an Associate Pastor at Pacific Beach United Methodist Church in San Diego, one of my roles was to be the minister of evangelism which mainly involved visiting people who attended the church for the first time. Pacific Beach is located between the Pacific Ocean and Mission Bay, so there were quite a few visitors. I worked with the Commission of Evangelism in the church. One of the members put forward an idea of stringing a fishing line across the porch of the church and as people joined having their names on a cut out of a fish suspended from a hook on the line. I had a little trouble dissuading him. It's a time for rejoicing when people come into the church but they are not hooked. When I was Chaplain at Somerville House, I had a visit in my office one morning from a student who attended an evangelical church who felt that I was missing my opportunity to "save" the girls by preaching that their only hope for eternal life was in believing in Jesus as Lord and Saviour. After congratulating her on having the courage to come and speak to me I explained that the model I took for my chaplaincy was provided by the words of Jesus, "I have come so that people might have life and have it in its fullness" that I hoped to provide guidelines for fuller life through Assembly worship, chapel services, and Religious Education, that I didn't want the students to feel that every time we met, I would be seeking to convert them. I think this is a good image for bringing in people, to be genuinely interested in them and concerned about them and if and when they ask, to explain what it means to us to follow Jesus, to be a Christian to attend church whatever the starting point. Amen

QUESTIONS

1. There is no doubt that progress has been made in some societies in acceptance and equal treatment of those of different sexual identities and those of other races but in both cases we are dealing with what can be engrained attitudes. If someone is sincere in committing to following Jesus then any prejudice needs to go. Do you have suggestions as to how an individual and/or a church can overcome prejudice?

2. The church throughout the centuries has in most areas reached out to the needy and oppressed. How would you rate your particular church in this regard? Are there areas where more concern and action could be applied?

3. There has been a good deal of emphasis in recent years on discipleship, particularly seeking to attract more disciples. In Point 3 a couple of approaches to seeking to carry this out are indicated which the writer obviously didn't agree with. What do you think? Can you think of anyone you have been able to interest in following Jesus? There is a low key approach outlined at the end of Point 3. What do you think of that?

Mark 1:29–32 Jesus healing Peter's mother-in-law and other people from Capernaum

Jesus and Healing

INTRODUCTION

In these verses Mark continues his account of the beginnings of Jesus's ministry. He visited Peter's house and healed Peter's mother-in- law who Mark said had a fever, and then a whole number of sick people who were brought to Peter's house. I feel this passage gives an opportunity to consider sickness and healing within the Christian faith, never an easy topic.

JESUS THE HEALER

In the three years of Jesus's ministry when he moved around Palestine, mostly in Galilee he carried out a number of healings. It was not uncommon at the time for those known as prophets, as Jesus was, to carry out healings as well as preach and teach. The news of his healing work spread and ensured that crowds came to see him and listen to him. There were, apparently those who practised medicine at the time. One commentator pointed out that Jesus did not use elaborate rituals in his healing. I think the greatest thing we can learn from the healings we've read about this morning and all the others is the deep concern Jesus had for the wellbeing of people. With this starting point, over the centuries, those who have sought to follow Jesus have most times shown similar concern. Hospitals and retirement homes originated with the church. However, that concern has been carried out with the backing of medical science and the medical profession. There have also, of course, been those who have endeavoured to follow more directly the practice of Jesus and seek to heal through such methods as laying on of hands. My personal feeling is that this has often led to misunderstanding and false expectation. In this passage from Mark a number of healings were reported through the casting out of "demons." It was, at the time, a common explanation for some illnesses, notably epilepsy. Our third son, Mark, who suffered brain damage through meningitis was and is subject to epilepsy. In our lifetimes we actually heard a minister report to a congregation that earlier in that week end he had taken part in a healing through the casting out of a demon of epilepsy. 2000 years ago, when Jesus walked the earth such a statement is understandable as when someone experiences an epileptic seizure it appears as if that person is being affected by something outside themselves. Medical science tells us that epilepsy is caused by some form of brain damage. Each week in worship we express our concern for the present and future wellbeing of a number of people. I believe we are catching them up into the concern of the congregation. I purposely don't pray specifically for their healing as it may or may not happen, rather that they might know strength and peace.

PAIN AND MORTALITY

As human beings we are mortal, that is, we have limited time on this "blue planet." We can to some extent, have an effect on how long that time will be, by attention to diet, exercise, and on our use of that time by following our interests, seeking to maintain and even develop intelligence. We will at some time in our lives, suffer pain. Because we are mortal when we are injured in some way or when various organs are not functioning the way they should, we will suffer pain. That pain can, of course, thankfully be alleviated thanks to the advances of medical science. All that may sound morbid, but I'm leading up to saying that to my knowledge there is no passage in the Bible which suggests that in seeking to follow Jesus we will be free of pain, or grief or loss. I think sometimes some may have the sense that in seeking to do the right thing and

JESUS AND HEALING

what Jesus wants they will live a somewhat charmed life. I want to repeat that is not the case. The next point follows quite naturally, the experience of pain and loss is completely random. Someone can bring disaster on themselves by for example drinking or taking other drugs and driving, or just over using drugs or taking unnecessary risks but when someone seems to be singled out by disaster it is a random event.

NOT WHY BUT HOW

Moving quickly on I'm not sure where I read or heard the next thing I'm going to say but I consider it extremely helpful when we are confronted by illness, disability or loss of any description. When we are in this situation the most important question is not why? but how? Not why did this happen to me, that is, if we aren't directly responsible, but how can I meet it and deal with it. Why? could lead to false accusations and bitterness, how, can lead to proceeding with life and maybe even lead to getting more from life. It is best to allow the individual to think through some situation themselves rather than prescribe some course of action or idea. I'm almost sure I came up with the next thing I'm going to say. When facing long term illness or disability there are two major steps, acceptance and adaptation. These are by no means small steps and may take a while to arrive at. Let's look at someone like Dylan Alcott, the wheel chair tennis player, affected in childhood but I'm sure we can all think of cases closer to us. Dylan Alcott, accepted his disability and then adapted to handling it. When we're seeking to follow Jesus, we're following someone who told and showed us how to get the most from life and when we join a church, the body of Christ, we discover a fellowship which provides support and guidance Amen

Jesus and Healing

QUESTIONS

1. How important to you is the acceptance of Jesus's healing miracles as being literally true? Whatever your response, why do you think that is the case?

2. Is your commitment to following Jesus, dependent on being free of pain and loss? Have you had to wrestle with this problem?

3. How helpful, if at all, are the ideas of asking not why? but how? when faced with pain and loss and when facing loss of any description seeking to follow the two steps, "acceptance" and "adaptation."

Mark 5:21–43 (Jesus healing daughter of Synagogue ruler and haemorrhaging woman)

Unlimited Compassion

INTRODUCTION

I don't often use the whole of a passage in a sermon but it seemed the best way to discover a main message from this particular passage. Our theme is "Unlimited Compassion" because I believe this is what Jesus showed in the incidents described by Mark. The pocket Macquarie Dictionary defines compassion as, 'a feeling of sorrow or pity for another; sympathy' which is the right idea but I think it could have stated, 'feeling with'. I need to acknowledge my heavy dependence on Rev. Dr William Barclay's great commentary on this passage. He was the lecturer in New Testament Language and literature at the University of Glasgow and published commentaries on all the books of the New Testament. I bought the whole series probably in about 1955 and they have been of enormous benefit.

BEYOND CLASS AND POSITION

The major part of the passage deals with a man called Jairus coming to ask Jesus to visit his daughter who was extremely ill, even close to dying. He felt sure that if Jesus touched her, she would get well. He was the person in charge of the synagogue. For some reason the 'Bible for Today' translates synagogue as 'Jewish meeting place'. Apparently, this meant that he was he administrative head of the synagogue, president of the board of elders who were responsible for its good management and was responsible for the conduct of the services. He didn't actually take part in the services but was responsible for the allocation of duties and seeing that they were carried out. As the ruler of the synagogue, he was one of the most respected men in the community. The extent of his concern for his daughter was shown in the extent of his plea to Jesus, going down on his knees. Jesus didn't hesitate but went with him with people crowded around the disciples and himself. Throughout the gospels it is made obvious that the officials of Judaism felt threatened by Jesus, especially when the people hung on his teaching enjoying its uniqueness and were impressed by the healings he did. Many times, the leaders tried to trap him in what he was saying in an effort to discredit him. None of this deterred Jesus when Jairus, the synagogue official asked for his help. He was driven by compassion since Jairus's great concern was obvious and there was a 12-year-old girl close to death. It was this attitude on the part of Jesus which led me to make 'Unlimited Compassion' our theme. Sometimes our feeling of compassion or the extent of it may be governed by our attitude to the people involved, maybe governed by different race, class or religion. This was not the case with Jesus.

A HUGELY AFFECTED WOMAN

There is another rather different incident tied in with Jairus's approach to Jesus. There was a woman in the crowd who had been haemorrhaging for 12 years. The account in Mark's gospel and it is also in Matthew and Luke says that she had been to a number of doctors who had not been able to help her. She was no doubt well known to the local people. Her condition would have meant that she was regarded as ritually unclean and she would need to avoid contact with others. There is a passage in Leviticus, 15: 19–30 which sets down necessary conduct for women with a similar condition and for a woman's periods. She had decided to take this opportunity to be healed and obviously was not planning to actually touch Jesus but probably one of the tassels on his outer garment, every Jewish male wore such a garment and it had a tassel at each corner. It was a sign that he was a member of the chosen people of God. Jesus was aware that someone had touched him and comments on it, which the disciples thought was not a sensible comment as there were people crowding in on them. He felt that power had gone from him, which is an interesting statement. Barclay makes the point that anyone who is leading a public event and focussing on it will feel drained but I think it was more than that. The woman was healed which must have been a profound relief but in the light of our theme, "Unlimited Compassion" it was remarkable that Jesus, who if he had followed the customs of Jewish males at the time wouldn't even have spoken to her, both spoke and seemed to have been undeterred at her touching him. His compassion transcended the restrictions. In these days when gender equality and identity is so much under discussion, it is good to check how limited our compassion may be in this regard.

AT THE BEDSIDE

As Jesus and the disciples continued to accompany Jairus to his house some people came from his house to let him know that his daughter had died so there was no point in continuing to involve Jesus. Jesus indicated that he still wanted to go to the house and got there to witness a scene of mourning with the professional wailers in full flight. He suggested that they were a bit ahead of themselves, as the little girl was just sleeping. There's been a lot of discussion about this. I've thought that when someone dies without a lot of pain it is like going into a permanent sleep but that the little girl may have been in a coma. We'll never know. There are two prime indications of Jesus's compassion. First of all he used the local language to speak to the girl, Aramaic, 'talitha koum', 'little girl, get up'. It showed understanding and affection. The second indication was Jesus suggesting that she be given something to eat, showing that he understood she may not have eaten for some time and a practical concern.

Compassion is an human emotion, other animals show affection and care within their own species but not outside it. When someone is affected by illness, accident or disaster, people respond out of their compassion, usually having experienced what the person is going through or at least appreciating their feelings. When we commit ourselves to following Jesus if we want to do so closely incidents such as the ones we have been considering let us know that we need to review our capacity for compassion. Humans are very tribal in terms of kin, race, colour, culture, religion but if we're following Jesus there should be no limit to our compassion and that is a challenge. Amen

QUESTIONS

1. It is natural for us to be more at home with people of our own race and even social status, as a follower of Jesus how can one work on their acceptance of people of other races and groups?

2. Women suffer discrimination in many countries around the world including our own and today with the LGBTQI situation there are other challenges. Jesus set a standard of acceptance 2000 years ago, how would you as an individual or as a group rate yourself/s?

3. How would you as an individual or as a group rate yourself in compassion? Is it limited in regard to race, nation, sex, or class?

Mark 10:14 "People who are like these little children belong to the Kingdom of God"

The Pluses of Being Children

INTRODUCTION

This is a beautiful little story and it tells us a great deal about Jesus and his attitudes. As someone pointed out children can be rather choosy as to who they wish to meet but it seems they were perfectly at home with Jesus as were the mothers who brought their children to be blessed.

THE CHILDREN

In the days of Jesus children did not have a prominent place in society. This was reflected in the attitude of the disciples who felt that for Jesus to give time to the children was a bother to him. In his response Jesus indicated that children were important to him. As happened time after time in his ministry Jesus showed he was not governed by the customs of his day and he saw the place of children.

Children are important, were then and are today. Time to time we are reminded that in what we do today in our decisions and policies we are deciding the future of the children of today and tomorrow. I think it is particularly in relation to climate change and attitude to the environment. Years ago, it was the natural expectation that a couple who married would endeavour to have children, if able. Today with the improvement in birth control methods more thought may be given. It is a huge responsibility bringing children into the world. When our first child, Paul was born and I think when I held him for the first time, out of the blue I thought, am I up for this? It was back in the days when a husband was not allowed anywhere near the birthing room, I have to say much to Mary's relief, she commented that she had enough to do giving birth without having to worry about her husband as well. There really is no direct training in bringing up children but in my efforts, I remember when backed into a corner using my parent's words or their attitudes. My observation of children in recent times is that at times in contrast to the days of Jesus they are allowed to be the centre and to assume that everything is their right so that finding the balance between thorough care and taking responsibility for their own attitudes is all important.

THE KINGDOM

Now a closer look at the verse we're focusing on. Jesus said, "people who are like these little children belong to the kingdom of God." The kingdom of God formed the major part of the teaching of Jesus. It was the theme of all his parables I'm sure he would have said this is my major goal in living to further establish God's kingdom. Not a particular place, or a particular group of people, not a racial group, a political group or a class. The kingdom is made up of those who are prepared to come under the rule of God and seek to do what God wants. We can be very thankful that we have the life, attitudes, and teaching of Jesus as an example of what God wants. At the centre is love, love to God, people, love to one another, that is, to those within the church, for it was to his disciples Jesus gave the new commandment to love one another. The kingdom is not one particular group of people but the church at its best is what the world should be when people do what God wants in terms of our trust and concern for one another and in reaching out to the world.

The Pluses of Being Children

CHILDLIKE

So to belong to the kingdom of God, that is, to feel accepted, to be getting the most out of life and giving the most to it we need to be childlike. I want to suggest just a few things that this may entail. The most important I believe is to have a sense of wonder, everything is new to a child and that may inspire a lot of questions which we may well not be able to answer but for us to continue to wonder is the alternative to becoming rather jaded, been there, done that and so on; b. to be open and accepting. This is the basic attitude of a child until influenced by the prejudice of many parents and prominent people; to be ready to learn, to be open to guidance, the best way to respond and of course that process never ends; c. to be resilient, there are many times in bringing up children when one feels they are mistaken in their responses and may wonder, what have I done? But children are resilient and seem to bounce back; d. to be trusting. I know one has to be careful, there are threatening people and situations but being trusting is vital to relationships; e. to move towards becoming independent, little children have to be dependent but the goal of growing up is to be independent. I believe that when Jesus called the early disciples to follow him, he was giving them a choice and they willingly decided to follow. There are many childlike qualities as outlined here which help one to belong to the kingdom of God but the foundational one involves our ongoing commitment to follow Jesus. Amen

QUESTIONS

1. Aristotle, the ancient Greek philosopher said, "Give me a child till he's 7 and I'll show you the man," meaning those early years are particularly formative. Are those words true in your experience? Children tend to absorb the attitudes and prejudices of those early years. How can that understanding shape early childhood education and even influence child rearing practices? In years gone by Sunday School and

church were well attended. As this is no longer the case what can the church do to attract children and young people or at least influence them?

2. The Kingdom of God or of Heaven was the core of Jesus's message but hasn't always been the core of the church's message. Any thoughts as to why? What would be an ideal representation of life if God's will, was done by the majority?

3. In Point 3 various meanings of childlikeness are given. People like that should make up the Kingdom of God. As you look at each meaning, how do you measure up?

Mark 13:36 "But if he comes suddenly, don't let him find you asleep. I tell everyone just what I have told you. Be alert!

Sleepless in Ipswich

INTRODUCTION

The "don't let him find you asleep" words having sparked off thoughts of the movie/ DVD "Sleepless in Seattle" meant that I had to buy the DVD and watch it. It's a real "feel good" romance. The wife of the male lead, Tom Hanks has died and his son, about 11 or 12 is very concerned about him as his father has great difficulty sleeping, amongst other things so the boy calls up a radio counsellor and tells her about his father. The counsellor names him, "Sleepless in Seattle." The lead lady, played by Meg Ryan who is in a rather unsatisfactory relationship hears the interviews and eventually they get together. I love a good "romance." But what has that to do with our text. Not a lot, I have to say, other than the "sleepless" idea. The main concern is that we need to be alert in our attitude to life and particularly the close following of Jesus.

END TIMES

Our Gospel passage comes under the heading of an apocalyptic writing, apocalyptic coming from the word "apocalypse" meaning revelation. There are two other examples of this form of writing in the Bible, Daniel in the Old Testament and Revelation in the New. There were many writings around the time of Jesus coming under the heading of "apocalyptic." As the heading for this point suggests they were to do with "end times." They suggest that time is moving towards a catastrophic ending which could be linked with a day of judgment. Those who have had visions of these endings, including in these words of Jesus suggest that this "end time" is frightening and it is a threat.

What is depicted in these ancient descriptions are phenomena of nature and of course, natural phenomena such as violent storms and earthquakes are destructive and scary. We have reached an age in the History of the world when humankind has become very capable of bringing about its own end. I'm thinking, of course, of nuclear and/or biological warfare. Someone has suggested a word I had never come across before to describe this age in which we live. It is "Anthropocene." He suggests that just as in the geologic ages which are shown in rocks and so on, this is an age which is shaped by human kind. There have been a number of books written which deal with a possible doomsday scenario if nations do resort to nuclear warfare or if human kind ignores the effect we are having on the planet. In a recent novel by David Baldacci I read I came across the term, "Doomsday preppies." I googled the term and discovered that there are people who have prepared themselves for a possible "doomsday" by building huge bunkers which are stocked to enable survival for a long period. In the novel I'm referring to a particular person had bought a disused silo built to house a rocket and transformed it into luxury "doomsday" accommodation.

Throughout the centuries from time to time there have been people who have felt that they have received a revelation from God specifying a time when all things will come to an end. They usually have no trouble attracting a number of followers.

NOBODY KNOWS

I'm very glad that Jesus in relation to when the end times he spoke of would come about said, "No one knows the day or the time. The angels in heaven don't know and the Son himself doesn't know. Only the Father knows." If we ever come across someone who is predicting a definite time for the world as we know it to end, we have every reason to be sceptical. Particularly if they are suggesting a pooling of resources or contributing to some sort of relief fund.

Sleepless in Ipswich
BEING ALERT

The on-going attitude which Jesus suggests is one of alertness. I don't think he meant that we should literally be wary of sleeping. I'm sure I don't need to go into details about the importance of sleep to our well-being. So how can we be alert or ready if our existence as we know it should come to an end. Throughout the centuries there have been people who have gone to extremes to endeavour to avoid contamination from the world. The one who stands out for me from my Church History days is Simon Stylites who spent years at the top of a pillar of rock. I'm not sure that spending hours and hours in prayer is the answer either. At the basis of it all is our commitment to following Jesus and seeking to ensure that our attitudes to those about us and life in general are in accord with what we know of him. A good guide to such attitudes is found in Paul's first letter to the Corinthians Chapter 13 in which he defines love, starting love is patient and kind. We will no doubt fail from time to time but as we have opportunity we need to apologise and start again. Every time we repeat the Lord's prayer, we are reminded of one ongoing need, "Forgive us our sins as we forgive those who sin against us." In other words, we need to avoid carrying grudges and wherever possible reach understanding with those with whom we have had a falling out. We need to remember that we are on the way, set down by Jesus. We are pilgrims as John Bunyan pointed out. We need reminders which is why the Church is so important and we are not in this alone we need to both give and be open to support. I can't think of any better way to finish than to repeat the challenge of John Wesley, "Do all the good you can, by all the means you can, in all the ways you can, in all the places you can, at all the times you can, to all the people you can, as long as ever you can."

QUESTIONS

1. Do you accept that there will be a cataclysmic, religious end to the world? Why? or Why not?
2. Even before the time of Jesus there was a belief that there would be a massive crisis in the world. Jesus also accepted this but at no specific time. Why do you think this belief has cropped up so repeatedly?
3. Are you awake? Alert? As Jesus suggested his followers should be? If you think you are what has got you to this state?

Luke 2: 52 "Jesus became wise, and he grew strong. God was pleased with him and so were the people."

Growing Towards Integrity

INTRODUCTION

This incident in the life of Jesus helps us to piece together what went on in his life from his birth, of which we know only a little till when he was 30 when he began his ministry. We're told that Mary and Joseph took him to Jerusalem for the observation of the Passover. This is the festival which remembers the final event which led to the release of the Jewish ancestors from slavery in Egypt. Jesus was 12 going on 13 so I wonder if this was his Bar Mitzvah a ceremony in which a boy becomes a "son of the commandment" and is regarded as entering adulthood.

JESUS AT 12

So we get a glimpse of Jesus at 12. We see a youth who was full of questions and on the verge of independence. It could be said he was pushing the boundaries when he stayed behind in Jerusalem. Anyone who has raised children or worked with them will know about the questions which seem to have a habit of keeping on coming. I believe it is one of the pluses of more recent times when generally children are encouraged to question. In earlier times when children were generally to be seen and not heard it could have been different. I always consider I went through adolescence in my 40's when I had opportunity to face up to all the questions and doubts which must have been accumulating in my mind.

Growing Towards Integrity

I don't think we give enough credit to Mary and Joseph in their bringing up of Jesus. Mary, of course, has always been given a special place but Joseph who it seems lived till Jesus was at least 20 has been neglected or ignored. Their attitudes must be reflected in those which Jesus displayed. Jesus would have attended school in the local synagogue being taught by the Rabbi the Jewish Scriptures which we call the Old Testament and with them to read and speak Hebrew. I'm sure he asked questions of his parents and the Rabbi but obviously he had questions which he had stored up and trotted them out when he had the opportunity in the temple at Jerusalem.

GROWING IN BODY AND MIND

So in this verse Luke comments that Jesus became wise and he grew strong, in other words he grew in body and mind and both God and the people were pleased with what they saw. They obviously felt that he was going places. We don't know how tall Jesus was or how well built but he did work as a carpenter and in later life mixed with hard working fishermen. It is a fact that as time has gone on the generations have tended to, in general, get bigger. I'm not sure what applied some 2000 years ago. I want to focus on growing in wisdom. Wisdom is more than knowledge. Knowledge is acquired through study, reading and observation but wisdom has the addition of experience and experience only comes through living and meeting varying circumstances. This is why older people are often regarded as being wise. It's how we meet and deal with these varying circumstances which can add to our wisdom. There is a beautiful prayer which helps with our approach, "God grant me the serenity to accept the things I cannot change. The courage to change the things I can and the wisdom to know the difference."

Growing Towards Integrity

A LIFETIME OF GROWING

In this final point I want to suggest that growing goes on for a life time, not in body, in fact as some of us will attest one tends to shrink somewhat with age but as those in the know tell us it is important to keep the body moving as much as possible. I want to refer at this stage to a psychiatrist by the name of Eric Erikson. He was in his heyday a couple of decades ago and followed Freud but went way beyond him in his ideas. He suggested that at various stages of our lives there are tasks we should be working on. In each case he suggested a scale with the lowest point of the particular task at one end and the peak of that task at the other. They start in infancy. The task at adolescence, identity vs role confusion. At young adulthood about 20–30, Intimacy vs isolation; at adulthood 30–50, generativity vs stagnation; in old age, ego integrity vs despair.

So we need some definitions: ego is, in effect one's person, who one is. I've always had trouble defining "integrity" but here goes with the aid of the Macquarie Concise Dictionary, "honesty, uprightness" and the one I really want, "the condition of being whole, or having it together." I believe being a follower of Jesus has everything to do with working through these tasks. Jesus came he said to help people find fullness of life. Following Jesus is a way of life, and leads to getting the most out of life and giving the most to it. In a passage from Colossians, words which Paul wrote to the people in the church at Colossae, he suggests what can be expected from people who are seeking to follow Jesus, "be gentle, kind, humble, meek and patient. Put up with one another, and forgive anyone who does you wrong, love is more important than anything else" and later: "be grateful." I think that's a good description of having integrity.

So as we remember Jesus at 12 and have a glimpse of his development it's a good opportunity to consider our own process of development where we're at and continue with keenness the Christian way. Amen

Growing Towards Integrity

QUESTIONS

1. Over the centuries as the life of Jesus has been read about in the Gospels, the likeness of his development to that of all of us has often been overlooked. Have you been or are you surprised that Jesus approaching adolescence had lots of questions? How do you handle children's and young people's questions, if you have opportunity, about belief, religion, life, in general?

2. If you happen to be getting up in years, do you notice any growth in wisdom? If younger do you notice that process in older people? Can you think of any facets of life and the environment that you know and/or understand more now or notice?

3. Whatever age you happen to be, how do you rate yourself against the description Paul thought could apply to someone seeking to follow Jesus as quoted in Colossians 3: 12–17

Luke 14:26 "You can't be my disciple, unless you love me more than you love your father and mother, your wife and children, and your brothers and sisters. You can't come with me unless you love me more than your own life."

Top Priority

Over the years people have put together a group of sayings of Jesus which they have labelled difficult, in some cases difficult to interpret and maybe also tough to carry out. I would list the words we're focussing on as fitting into both categories particularly as it happens to be one of the lectionary readings for Father's day. A day in which I choose to pay attention to the family. If we follow out what Jesus said I believe families finish off better off.

THE IMPORTANCE OF FAMILY

Jesus was by no means putting families down. With his own family, certainly there is a time recorded, when, showing that they hadn't understood his mission they tried to take him home feeling he was probably making a fool of himself when he basically ignored them and indicated his family was really the people he spoke to from day to day—Mark 3:31–35. However, as a Jew he would have grown up following the commandment to "Honour his father and mother." In the midst of his agony on the cross he remembered that his mother would need caring for having lost her husband and her oldest son. The family is the most important unit in society. I'm thinking of our own society but the same applies in most societies around the world. I know there are still some societies which practise polygamy but they are also ones in which there is male dominance. When I say the family is the most important unit in society I'm thinking monogamy, one wife, one husband and where there is complete equality between the partners. I'm well aware of the amount of flux there is in our society at the moment to do with definition of a family but I'm not planning to deal with that flux in any detail as I think it would be a distraction as we consider this passage. The family is important mainly because it is society in miniature. It contains a balance of male and female and in an ideal situation with neither seeking to dominate. There is the possibility of children and those children come into the world with a mixture of genes from both parents. They don't come into the world with the innate ability to know right from wrong or how best to treat other people or themselves for that matter but in an ideal sense they are in the best position to learn all this as they gradually become aware of their parents and possibly brothers and sisters. It's often been observed that our education system has an absolute plethora of subjects designed to widen our knowledge and to train us to think and reason but mostly there is no discussion of how best to bring up children. In my time teaching Religious Education at Somerville House—a Uniting Church Presbyterian Girls' School, we did attempt to give time to discussion of forming relationships and marriage but Year 12 students had a lot of other things on their minds and some thought marriage would be the last gasp. There were times in bringing up our own children that in some situations I found myself recalling how my parents dealt with me even as far as using the same expressions. We can't afford as a society or a church to neglect the place of family.

PUTTING JESUS FIRST

Now to look more closely at these words of Jesus. At first glance it seems that what Jesus was saying is completely mystifying. If people are asked what is most important in their lives, they will say family but Jesus is saying I give you a higher priority, put more importance on following me. In King's College while training for the ministry back in the days when we weren't permitted to marry until ordained as we discussed this, we considered this meant that the church should come before wife and possibly children. This meant in our first Circuit my being out six nights a week and on the other night preparing a sermon. That was excessive and fortunately I was married to a long-suffering wife. To love Jesus more than anything else is to make following him the most important thing in our lives. To place ourselves on the way of life he set down by his teachings and attitudes. Very often the testing ground for the success or otherwise of following Jesus is in family relationships where one is known "warts and all." We come together in a relationship through romantic love and the world would be the poorer and less exciting without it. In an on-going relationship of any description, if it is to be worthwhile, it needs a large slice of the sort of love Jesus and Paul spoke about. Commitment to one another is the basis and Paul defined it in his first letter to the Corinthians "love is patient, kind, never boastful, proud or rude, not selfish or quick tempered, doesn't keep a record of wrong, always supportive, loyal" (13:4-8). It's a lot to live up to but to put Jesus first is to give ourselves maximum chance of success and fortunately forgiveness is an option.

THE FAMILY OF HUMANKIND

In this third and last point I want to extend our family vision beyond a household to the family of humankind and even beyond that to all that has life. If we do give Jesus top priority then we will seek to show the sort of love I've referred to, to family but our concern and compassion will not be limited we are part of a much, much bigger family the human race. We think our families are varied and made up of very different individuals which is exciting and challenging but think of the family of human kind. The variety is incredible race, culture, religion, degrees of wealth from the very rich to those with abject poverty. Jesus did say the second most important commandment is to love people as you love yourself. He didn't specify one race, or people of one nation. I think the largest part of such love has to be concern. We have no right if we're seeking to follow Jesus to write anyone off or even worse to consider anyone expendable. Just quickly I believe we need to extend our family to all that has life. Humankind has been

Top Priority

too quick and thoughtless in exploiting other forms of life. I think Francis of Assisi had the right idea when he personalised various parts of nature. I know this is a very idealised picture but it's one that provides hope. Amen

QUESTIONS

1. What does family mean to you? If this question is being considered in a group, there may be a number of different situations. I'd like to suggest the question be dealt with sensitively. Do you think there is sufficient attention to family values in our society?

2. Do you think the old marriage vows are outmoded, that is," for better or worse, for richer or poorer, in sickness and in health, till death do us part."? If so, what would be a good substitute?

3. The human race a family? Pipe dream? What needs to happen for this to approach coming about? Do you talk to the birds, perhaps the trees and flowers? How important to you are all forms of life?

Luke 15:7 *"There is more happiness in heaven because of one sinner who turns to God than over 99 good people who do not need to."*

Repentance is the Way to Go

INTRODUCTION

Jesus used parables a great deal to get his message across. Back in the days when those going to Sunday School could be asked to learn a catechism question and answer as well as verses from the Bible, a parable was defined as "an earthly story with a heavenly meaning." I like to think of them as stories with a punch line. In this chapter in Luke's Gospel he recorded Jesus using three parables on the same theme. They were all sparked off by the grumblings of some of the Jewish religious leaders to do with Jesus attracting and associating with people the leaders regarded as sinners. The older versions of the Bible use the word "repent" where the Bible for Today uses "turn to God." I like the word "repent" as I believe it gives the impression of a more emphatic change.

SELF-RIGHTEOUSNESS TO BE AVOIDED

The Pharisees who are mentioned in the Gospel reading belonged to a sect of the Jews who followed the laws of the then Jewish religion very strictly. This was not just the ten commandments but rules governing every detail that might arise. For example, following out the observance of the Sabbath to the extent of not seeking the well-being of the sick on that day which was one of their criticisms of Jesus healing a woman in the Synagogue. The Pharisees did not associate with those who did not have their strict attitude to the observance of the law. This is a good example of self-righteousness a sense of extreme satisfaction at one's own stance, in terms of faith and values, a cut above everyone else. Jesus is our best example here of an opposite attitude. Certainly, Christian doctrine regards Jesus as being without sin but on one occasion he objected to being called good. He mixed with people and enjoyed being with them with concern for their needs and wanting their well-being. To be ready to follow Jesus or be a disciple is to seek to be the best that we can be and to give the most that we can to life but not to have a sense of superiority.

REPENTANCE, THE WAY TO GO, A BEGINNING

The punch line in these parables is the party thrown at the highest level when someone repents. If one asks is there something wrong with trying to be good then the point is being missed. Jesus definitely wasn't suggesting that there's anything wrong with being kind and loving. The dictionary definition of repentance tends to stress being sorry for wrong doing that one may have been involved in and that is definitely a factor as if a person has no sense of right and wrong and is not aware of being hurtful, then there will be no desire to change. Years ago, I came across an explanation of repentance which I think is emphatic and clear. It is a U-turn in one's life. It was a monthly occurrence years ago for many young Methodists from around Brisbane to meet in Albert Hall next to Albert Street church for Methodist Youth Fellowship. There would probably have been 3-4 hundred there which was very inspiring. At every gathering two young people would give testimonies, their faith journey, if you will. I can remember that sometimes it seemed that there could be a struggle to show how much of a change had come about in their lives when they committed those lives to Jesus. In other words, like myself they had most likely grown up in Christian homes and been a part of the church. They most likely had not become addicted to alcohol nor back then, drugs or had a gambling habit, or embarked on a life of burglary, or embezzlement or beaten anyone up. The point was and is that whatever background one might have it is the commitment one makes to follow Jesus which is all important. Certainly, if one comes from a background like Paul, who called himself, the "chief of sinners," the change in one's life is very obvious, but it's not a good use of time to blacken one's past.

THE NEED FOR REVIEW

The three parables in this chapter of Luke, the lost sheep, coin and son, spell out that God wants a person to be "found," to be on a good course in life. Jesus spelt that out when he said that he was in the world so that people would discover life in its fullness. The repentance Jesus speaks about is a first step or a milestone, a finding of forgiveness, a beginning, there's yet the rest of life. I become a little impatient when I meet a person who is very assured that they have it made as to their life now and to all eternity. It's far more humbling to have a sense that one has a way to go to reach perfection. I grew up in the Methodist Church and trained for the Methodist ministry. I therefore became very familiar with the emphases of the Wesleys, John and Charles. Two of those emphases were "sanctification," seeking greater holiness and "Christian Perfection" being the best possible person in terms of faith, hope and love. Personally, I have trouble believing in perfection. I don't think it's possible. John Wesley said on one occasion that perfection in love was possible. I'm not sure his wife would have agreed. All that is a prelude to saying that when we "repent," being committed to following Jesus, we're on the way, the way Jesus established in his life and it's a great and satisfying way, but it's a work in progress if we really are committed. Amen

QUESTIONS

1. How does one become aware of a sense of self-righteousness and how does one overcome it?
2. If you are reading this sermon by yourself recall what led you to the state of belief you have now? If this is part of a

group exercise, share individual experiences and awareness of change as one seeks to follow Jesus.

3. Is the Christian perfection the Wesleys espoused ever a possibility and what, if anything would be the advantage?

Luke 18:9-14 The Parable of the Pharisee and the Tax Collector

A Searching but Honest View of Self

INTRODUCTION

One of the favourite methods Jesus used to get his point across was in telling stories which have been called Parables. The old catechism defined them as, "an earthly story with a heavenly meaning." They all really had just one meaning and in this case Luke spells it out, "Jesus told a story to some people who thought they were better than others and looked down on everyone else." You'll note that even though I pretty well always have three points in a sermon there are only two in this one, but don't get your hopes up it gives me more opportunity to expand on each point.

THE WORST FORM OF PRIDE

Pride is listed as one of the "7 deadly sins" and the old saying has it, "pride goeth before a fall." To be generally proud forces one into oneself and cuts off consideration of others and the saying suggests that to be proud really tempts fate and sets one up to make mistakes. In this parable we're considering one of the characters is a Pharisee, a member of a Jewish group who lived exemplary lives according to a great number of rules but could become pretty self-righteous as exaggerated by Jesus in the parable as he prayed. I've called this the worst form of pride because it contradicts the purpose of seeking to live a good worthwhile life through one's belief. Living out one's belief is meant to make life better for other people and oneself but to be satisfied with one's level of devotion or holiness is to tend to shut oneself off to others and maybe the world. The form of self-righteousness which I have most encountered is in those who consider themselves, "saved" which I think means that they consider they've got it made to all eternity, because at some time they have acknowledged Jesus as Lord. They are very likely to approach others with the question, "Are you saved?" At one time William Temple who was Archbishop of Canterbury was asked that question. He replied, "I was saved, I am being saved, I hope to be saved," which highlights the point that when we commit ourselves to following Jesus, we seek to adopt the way of life set out by Jesus in life and attitudes. Jesus said on one occasion, "Not everyone who calls me, Lord, Lord will enter the Kingdom of Heaven, but only those who do the will of my heavenly father." The emphasis, I believe, being on doing.

HUMBLE BUT NOT TOO HUMBLE

In this parable by contrast to the Pharisee, the tax collector couldn't even raise his eyes and pleaded to God for mercy. From all accounts tax collectors at the time were notorious for taking in more than the actual tax and siphoning off a good portion for themselves. Apart from that, they were mostly Jews but worked for the Romans, the nation who were in control at the time. Particularly in his parables Jesus used exaggeration to get his point across and probably boosted the level of the tax collector's penitence. I'm now going to commit, "hymnal heresy" and say that in spite of its popularity I don't like singing, "Amazing grace." It's because of the first verse, "Amazing Grace (how sweet the sound) that saved a wretch like me." I may not be an absolute paragon of virtue but I don't think of myself as a "wretch." John Newton the writer of the hymn had been a slave trader. He had a religious experience and became a changed man. He really was then no longer a wretch. I also don't go as far as the Psalmist who wrote, "But I am merely a worm, far less than human." (Psalm 22:6) I have a healthy respect for worms and what they do and got to the stage as my liking for fishing declined of not being able to put one on a hook but I don't

A Searching but Honest View of Self

go along with the Psalmist. It's really no advantage to put ourselves down. I'm not sure that that is even true humility. Paul wrote in his letter to the Romans (12:3) "I bid everyone among you not to think of himself more highly than he ought to think," thereby suggesting that it's OK to have a good regard for one's own qualities. The same sentiment is echoed in the second commandment which Jesus said was the greatest when he was asked once. These were ancient Jewish commandments, "Love others as much as you love yourself." Thereby OK'ing loving oneself. In other words, recognising one's own value. In recent decades Human Relationships or Values education has coined the expression, "self-esteem." I consider it is basic and essential for each individual to come to a point where they see their value, self-acceptance if you like. It's basic to worthwhile life and living. There is an exercise which is very useful in working towards good self-esteem. I've used this with a number of groups both young people and adults. Participants are asked to write down 5 negative things about themselves and 5 good qualities that they have. Almost invariably they will immediately write down the 5 negative things but have to sit and think a great deal about their good qualities. When we are seeking to follow Jesus, we are following someone who had great insights many of them from the Jewish faith he grew up in, whose positive attitudes were of interest in and acceptance of people no matter what nation, race, sex, religion they were, who had compassion particularly for those with various needs. We will have failed in our responses to people at times, and possibly we will continue to do so from time to time but forgiveness is there for the taking. We are different in appearance and personality but without exception we are of great worth and have a contribution to make to life and the world. Amen

QUESTIONS

1. Do you see advantages in seeing being committed to following Jesus as a way of life? If so, what are they, If not, why not.

A Searching but Honest View of Self

2. What do you feel is the attraction to many people of the hymn, "Amazing Grace." Do you consider the author of these questions to have committed "hymn heresy" in his dislike of singing about himself as a wretch?

3. You are invited to carry out the exercise in self-esteem set out towards the end of the second point. Perhaps, if in a group you could share possible difficulties or opinions.

Luke 22:14-20 The last supper Jesus had with his disciples

The Lord's Supper

INTRODUCTION

I think it's valuable from time to time to spend more time to consider the Lord's Supper in the time given to the sermon. I've made it a practice over the years on a Communion Sunday to try to relate whatever passage of the Bible is being considered to the practise of Holy Communion. Here we're considering the institution of the Sacrament. The passage which was just read indicates that the holding of this last meal together with the disciples was not a spur of the moment thing. Jesus had made plans as to the place of meeting. It was the Jewish Passover meal and it would be a normal thing for families to observe the ceremony in their own place of dwelling but Jesus and the disciples had no such place.

THE CENTRAL SERVICE OF THE CHURCH

I think the words Jesus used as he broke the bread and handed it to his disciples, "this is my body which is given for you. Eat this as a way of remembering me" indicate what he had in mind as he ate with them. It was a way of remembering that he had lived among them, that he had been amongst people as one of us. The observance of this symbolic meal became known as a sacrament, an outward sign of a deeper meaning and this began to be observed in the early church and has become the Central service of the church universal. I doubt very much if when Jesus initiated this meal he would have had any idea of the multiplicity of churches

The Lord's Supper

which would come to exist in the world and without exaggeration there are 100's. I think it's valuable to be aware of the various names which have been given to the Sacrament of the Lord's Supper in various churches and the different ways of observance. In doing so we need to remember that the unifying fact is that somewhere in the ritual the words of institution used by Jesus will be stated.

We'll start from the more ornate ways of observance and then mention some others. The Orthodox Churches use a rather elaborate ritual in buildings which are themselves ornate with a great number of icons depicting the apostles and other saints. I said Orthodox churches as the Orthodox version of the faith and its rituals are named in accord with the nations or territories in which they exist so for example, Greek, Russian and Serbian orthodox. The reciting of the ritual is extremely important and the priest is expected to repeat it exactly as written and this will be checked periodically during the visit of a Bishop or Archbishop.

The Catholic Church calls its observance of the Sacrament, the Mass. I looked up the derivation of the word in Dictionaries and even googled. Apparently, it arose in the 6th century and most likely comes from the concluding words "ite missa est" "go, the dismissal is made."

This also is an elaborate ritual and it is believed that at a certain point in the service the elements of Communion become the body and blood of Christ. This is rather hard to accept for Protestants including this one but it has a long tradition and I'm sure stems from the words of Jesus, this is my body and this is my blood.

Since the Lutheran church came directly from the Catholic there is a large use of symbolism in their churches. There is the belief that during the sacrament the actual presence of Christ is alongside or with the elements.

The Anglican Church also has a fairly elaborate ritual and the service is usually referred to as the Eucharist which means thanksgiving.

All the churches I have mentioned observe the sacrament as their regular form of worship, in other words each week, and will usually use wine.

The Lord's Supper

Most other churches including this one, that is, Uniting, observe the Sacrament of the Lord's Supper once a month. I think this came about to seek to make its observance special and to avoid repetition.

In the Presbyterian Church the Sacrament of the Lord's Supper is observed every three months. Elders visit the members and distribute cards.

Sadly, I believe, it used to be the case in some churches that those who were not members could not partake in the observance of communion in that church. This was against everything that Jesus taught and lived out. Fortunately these restrictions have been removed in recent years.

THE PLUSES OF HOLY COMMUNION

I think it is reassuring to realise that in spite of different practices across the churches there is in all of them the commonality of the creeds and this central sacrament. In this point I want to suggest how this service may help us as we seek to follow Jesus. I mentioned earlier as Jesus broke the bread and passed it round, he asked that his disciples eat it and remember him. So, as we participate in his sacrament, we are reminded that Jesus walked the earth and that we are following someone who as one of us established a way of life for us to follow. As Jesus passed the cup around, he said, "This is my blood. It is poured out for you and with it, God makes his new agreement." As we participate, we are reminded that we are accepted and that forgiveness is available for any shortcomings in our actions and relationships. Over the years people have at times been reluctant to participate in Communion because they don't feel good enough or are not worthy but this table, thanks to Jesus is open to all and can signal a new beginning.

As we eat and drink together, we are involved in a common act and are further bound together. There is a sense also that as we eat and drink we are carrying out an act which is observed across the whole church whatever the denominations are called and whatever name is used in that church. I like to think that since we are being linked anew to Jesus who was one of us and called himself the Son of man, we are being linked to the whole human race, whatever colour, nation, belief they may be.

One meaning of sacrament is an oath or pledge. A sacramentum was the pledge of service a Roman Soldier made to the emperor. As we share in this sacrament it is an opportunity to renew our commitment to following Jesus. We are following the way Jesus set down in his life. A plus is that we do this in the fellowship of a church. We are in this together and can support each other on the way. Amen

QUESTIONS

1. The diversity of forms of worship and church organisation across Christendom is astounding. Do you foresee any possibility of there ever being one Christian church? Any suggestions as to what would need to occur for it to happen? What about greater co-operation, do you have some ideas?

2. Does your church have an open Lord's table, that is, all persons may participate? If so, are you happy with the arrangement. If not, would you like to see it change? b. Do you have a certain frame of mind as you come to Communion? Early in his life the writer struggled to feel any greater sense of "presence" or inspiration. What about you? For the writer the deepest meaning is the reminder that Jesus did walk the earth and the service is an opportunity to realign oneself to the way he established. What do you think?

John 2:1-11 The Wedding at Cana of Galilee

Let's Celebrate

INTRODUCTION

We need to fill in the background on this wedding we're attending with Jesus in Cana of Galilee. It seems that Jesus had been invited to the wedding as had his mother but the family may not have known about the number of Jesus's disciples who would be coming with him causing a problem in the catering. It also seems that Mary had some sort of responsibility for the arrangements, maybe she was related. She certainly felt that Jesus could do something about the wine running out. It's an interesting response which Jesus makes to his mother. "Mother, you must not tell me what to do." Remember Jesus would have been about 30 and would probably have been the man of the house as the oldest in the family after Joseph seems to have died. It reminds me that parents have trouble recognising that their off spring have become adults. We still refer to Paul and Stephen who are 64 and 62 as our boys. I seem to remember as I was growing up in the Methodist church ministers having trouble with the fact that there were large quantities of wine at this celebration. There really shouldn't have been a problem as red wine is a definite part of Jewish ceremonial let alone celebrations.

THE SIGNS

At the beginning of verse 11 John wrote, "This was Jesus's first miracle." Earlier translations of the Bible have "sign" rather than miracle and apparently this is more correct. William Temple,

Archbishop of Canterbury, 1942–44, Scholar and author lists the 7 signs indicated in John's gospel and what they meant. Included are the "feeding of the 5000." The turning of water into wine he suggests points to the "difference Jesus makes." If we take that to mean the water being turned to wine, then it is quite a difference. Each of the 6 jars which were there for the Jewish ritual washing which were refilled contained 100 litres, so that's a fair bit of wine. In his parables Jesus loved using hyperbole or exaggeration and perhaps what happened at the wedding feast is an example. So, what difference does following Jesus make. To the individual it gives one's life an overall purpose. Thanks to our different aptitudes and interests we find our way into different occupations and situations and relationships but when we're following Jesus the attitudes we adopt are guided by his attitudes and teaching. To the community at large he seeks to bring justice and peace and harmony. The core of his teaching was and is, "The Kingdom of God," the rule of God, not in the sense of an actual Kingdom or empire but people of good will seeking justice for all. The church of which we are a part and which was set up with his early disciples and continues with his disciples modelling their lives and attitudes on the life of Jesus has a huge responsibility. Our congregation is a small part of the kingdom and is to demonstrate the difference Jesus makes.

CELEBRATE WHAT?

We've been talking about accompanying Jesus to a wedding, but, of course, this isn't a wedding breakfast, but I hope we're in celebration mode, but celebrating what? First, an aside, there have been periods throughout its history when at least parts of the church, have I believed been rather puritanical in their attitudes and have applied unnecessary restrictions. I believe this has been a misreading of what Jesus was on about who was accused by some of being a wine drinker in contrast to John the Baptist who lived as a hermit for much of his life. I grew up in the Methodist church where there was a restriction on dancing on church property. Really that was to my advantage as I seem to have two left feet, however, in our church socials we really did have rather riotous times, end of aside. First of all, in any celebration we need to celebrate living. We're alive, we've entered this new day with all its possibilities, the possibilities will vary according to our interests and tastes. Maybe we're not dancing in the aisles, and I'm afraid, speaking personally I'm not given to excessive displays, but we have our individual ways, feeling content, breaking into whistling along with music we like. Church services almost invariably give opportunity for what could be lovely singing. We've already spoken about the difference Jesus makes so we celebrate following Jesus as closely as possible in his very positive and life shaping attitudes. I'm convinced that we need to have activities or events we look forward to. It doesn't have to be earth shattering, it may be a meeting with family or friends, an excursion. We can celebrate being here, our association with the church. Many or most of us have a very long-term association. Sometimes students at Somerville House in an R.E. period would ask me why I went into the ministry. I'd reply that the church was my life that on Sundays I went to Christian Endeavour at 10am, Church at 11am, Sunday School at 3pm., maybe a Fellowship tea and then church at 7.30 pm. In addition, Youth Group on a Friday night, tennis on the church courts on Saturday afternoons, maybe a Youth rally on a Saturday night and Camps in some holidays and as their mouths dropped open, I'd conclude by saying and mostly I loved it. For those who have not been involved in the church the impression they have is that it is dreary, restricting. We can't afford to let that happen and I don't believe we have. It's a place for fellowship, learning more about the Christian way, mutual support, contributing to the world which Jesus wanted and wants, of justice, peace, compassion and tolerance. Amen

QUESTIONS

1. What difference, if any, to one's possible attitudes and interests does following Jesus make?

2. Is there any advantage to a "puritanical" attitude to life following Jesus?

3. How do you think one who is seeking to follow Jesus can best celebrate life?

John 6:35 "I am the bread of life. No one who comes to me will ever be hungry. No one who has faith in me will ever be thirsty."

The Stuff of Life

INTRODUCTION

The verse we're focussing on is one of a number in John's gospel which have the same format, starting with "I am," a couple of others being, "I am the water of life" and "I am the vine, you are the branches." It's suggested they hark back to the occasion when Moses is unsure what he is going to tell the captive Israelites in Egypt who had sent him to set them free. The puzzling answer was to say that "I am" has sent you." It's at least another whole sermon to try and interpret what was meant but when John uses the words in relation to Jesus it gives them the highest possible importance.

A STAPLE DIET

I want to try here to state what I think Jesus was meaning in these telling words. Bread has been called the staff of life because across the centuries in many societies it is a staple of the diet. In our society with a multiplicity of food lines this is not so obvious but most households would eat at least some bread every day. I think the big exception in what is regarded as staple diet would be SE Asian countries where the staple food is rice. The first thing that has to be stated is that Jesus was not just meaning actual bread. Having said that he made plain on a few occasions that he knew bread or actual food was a basic need for life. Two examples are in the incident of the feeding of the 5000, or actually nearly 10,000 as only men are mentioned in the gospel accounts. There Jesus was

The Stuff of Life

aware that the crowd hadn't eaten and Philip mentioned the lad who had loaves and fishes for his lunch. Also, after the daughter of Jairus was healed he suggested she be given something to eat. But you might be saying, he is recorded as saying that people who believe in him won't need anything else to sustain them. Jesus loved hyperbole and I believe this is a good example. He was stressing that to discover quality life people needed to believe in him. What in Jesus's terms is quality life. I want to put forward a few ideas. First of all, I would put, life with positive purpose, not just existing, although, of course that is absolutely basic, that is more than accumulating capital and all that goes with it, that goes beyond self-satisfaction, although I'm not discounting the importance of self-esteem, that therefore takes into account the importance of others and their needs and this includes all forms of life. I guess what I'm suggesting is finding an overall purpose in living which is seeking to follow Jesus, who thankfully in his life and attitudes laid down a way of life.

REGULAR INTAKE

When we're talking about food, we know that to sustain life we need to regularly partake. In a little aside I want to point out what just occurred to me as more than a little inconsistency. On one hand media regularly points out the perils of obesity and over eating but on the other has a preponderance of programmes to do with what are often very appealing meals to consume end of aside. Given that Jesus wasn't just talking about the place of bread and food sustaining life but rather things like purpose, attitudes, concerns and being like him in his way of life how do we go about getting onto this sort of diet. There are a number of hymns which suggest the Bible as the "bread of life. I'm not quarrelling with that as long as we don't forget that Jesus referred to himself as the "bread of life" and the Bible needs to be seen as providing the background to that fact in the Jewish scriptures and the aftermath in all the writings which come after the gospels. I think John made that plain in his gospel when he referred to Jesus as the Word, so then with that in mind the Bible is a Word of God not the Word. Having said that, I believe it is important to be familiar with the Bible and to ponder the meaning of what we are reading. This is why publications such as "With love to the World" are so useful with suggested readings for each day and with comments to help our understanding. Being a part of a study group is also very helpful as long as one opinion is not given dominance, but all opinions given a place. Being a part of the church, the "body of Christ," is also important in the sense that there is the effort of a particular person to help with the understanding of some part of scripture but above all is the reinforcement that we are all pilgrims on the way and need to support one another.

THE INESCAPABLE CONNECTION TO THE LORD'S SUPPER

Scholars have pointed out for a long time that these words and the verses around them are John's effort to put forward what the other Gospel writers wrote about, the sharing with the disciples in the last supper before his death and the calculated introduction of what the church came to call, Holy Communion, Lord's Supper, Mass, Eucharist, Breaking of Bread. Thanks to the multiplicity of denominations, there are varying methods of observance but all stem from the action of Jesus. John's recording of the words of Jesus in this connection are very telling. Jesus called himself, "the bread of life" To take part in this sacrament is to bind ourselves to Jesus, so to speak, and his way of life and find fresh incentive and motivation and in our sharing in the elements to realise again that we're in this together and we need one another. Amen.

QUESTIONS

1. How do you see the relation of Jesus as "the Word" and the Bible as the "word of God."

2. Towards the end of Point 1 there is an attempt to outline the benefits of following Jesus or what is involved in the quality of life realised in that following. Do you think what is suggested is adequate? What could be added?

John 15:12-13 "Now I tell you to love one another as I have loved you. The greatest way to show love for friends is to die for them."

It's Love, Love, Love

INTRODUCTION

With a theme like, "It's love, love, love" one could expect an R-rated sermon but I'm sorry to possibly cause disappointment. There's no doubt that love is mentioned many times in the Gospels and the letters, particularly in John's but it does not refer to romantic love which understandably occupies so much space in the media in general. I know what I'm about to say has been said time and time again from the pulpit but it has to be said. There is more than one word for love in Greek, the language in which the New Testament is written. The word for romantic love is eros, for family love philia, for desire epithumia. The word Jesus uses for love in this verse is agape. It really means ongoing respect and concern for people. It has the elements in it which Paul included in his great definition in his first letter to the Corinthians kindness, patience, forgiveness, trust, loyalty, unselfishness, unwillingness to boast. When couples choose the Corinthian's passage for weddings, I make a point of saying that even though romantic love brings a couple together there's no hope of a long term relationship without a large slice of the sort of love Jesus and Paul spoke about and the same applies to love within families. An important thing about this sort of love is that one can be committed to loving in this way. It's not something that comes and goes or depends on love being returned. Erich Fromm in his book, "The Art of Loving" objects to the term, "falling in love" on the understanding that one can just as easily fall out of love. In relationships he prefers the phrase, "standing in love."

It's Love, Love, Love

SEE HOW THESE CHRISTIANS LOVE ONE ANOTHER

When the early Christians were suffering horrendous persecution under some of the Roman emperors at the time, it is said that as people watched the Christians going to death their support for one another led observers to say, "See how these Christians love one another." There have been times in the history of the Christian church when that comment has been made in derision since there have been times of bitter disputes over points of doctrine or church organisation. Or there have been times on a local level when there has been obvious ill feeling amongst people in a congregation over what could be petty details. Given the passage we're considering and its blunt summing up by Jesus, "So I command you to love each other" it is very bad form indeed when the comment is made in derision rather than in reality. When one is committed to following Jesus, while it is an individual response, it is not one which has to be made in isolation, the church is there to provide support and constant fresh motivation if it is really functioning. When we are committed to following Jesus the process in following his way of life , thankfully, is a group one, we are pilgrims on the way. When we find our way into a particular congregation we won't like everyone, human personality and character is such that that is an impossibility but as Jesus commanded we can love everyone one, given the definition of the love Jesus was speaking about. There is a legend which grew up about the aging apostle John. He lived to a great age and became so feeble he had to be carried to meetings. Because of his weakness, he was unable to deliver a long message, so at each gathering he simply repeated the words, "Little children, love one another." The disciples, weary of hearing the same words over and over, asked him why he never said anything else. And to them, John gave this answer, "Do this alone and it is enough."

It's Love, Love, Love

JESUS, THE EXEMPLAR

It's very telling that according to John, at the time Jesus commanded his disciples to love one another, he added, "as I have loved you." He wasn't insisting on them doing anything he hadn't done himself. Sadly, there isn't a lot in the Gospels about the relationship between Jesus and the disciples. We know he appreciated their varied personalities, their strengths and weaknesses. So it was that Peter, Andrew, James and John seem to have become leaders and they accompanied Jesus when he went up a mountain before the experience which has become known as "the transfiguration" and when he went aside in the Garden of Gethseminane, to pray before the crucifixion. Also he called James and John, "the sons of thunder." They were obviously rather mercurial. However, he did say that he loved them.

IT'S TO DIE FOR

In the last few phrases of the verses we're focussing on, John records Jesus as saying, "the greatest way to show love for friends is to die for them." It is a very true statement, there can be no greater way. Those words have, of course, always been applied to Jesus's own action in going to his own death. They have also been read at many Anzac Day services and are very applicable to those who gave up their lives to defend our freedom and perhaps in direct defence of their mates. There are countless examples throughout history of people giving their lives for the sake of loved ones and friends. The expression has also found its way into more regular use when someone says something, event or object was "to die for." I believe we can apply that idea to current gatherings of disciples. I believe this is or definitely should be what makes the fellowship we find in the church even better than the good feeling we have in any group. In the church we are commanded to love one another and I plead with you to remember the definition of the love, Jesus spoke about. We have a right here to be respected, accepted and the recipients of ongoing concern. Just one final point, the commitment has to be mutual, others in the church have a right to expect this sort of love from each of us. Another reminder, Jesus enjoined us to show this sort of love to all people, our neighbours no matter what race, culture, class or religion and of course, as much as we show that love to ourselves. Amen

QUESTIONS

1. Most, if not all ministers as a part of their training study New Testament Greek as the original language of the New Testament, "common usage" Greek as opposed to classical Greek. Have you found it useful to learn that there are three words for love in Greek? If so, what help did you find?

2. "See how these Christians love one another," said as early Christians were martyred. In what ways could a modern congregation be exemplars of mutual support?

3. It may not be possible to like everyone but it could be possible to love everyone, nonsensical? How could it be sensible?

4. What has been your experience when visiting other congregations or seeking to become members? Did you find welcome? What impression does being commanded to love one another make on you, favourable or not?

John 17:20–21 "I am not praying just for these followers. I am also praying for everyone else who will have faith because of what my followers will say about me. I want all of them to be one with each other, just as I am one with you and you are one with me. I also want them to be one with us. Then the people of this world will believe that you sent me"

The Church Uniting

INTRODUCTION

The verses we're concentrating on are part of the great prayer of Jesus towards the end of his life. Because the prayer includes the words, "I am also praying for everyone else . . ." we can recognise that we are included in the prayer as was everyone else who has become a follower of Jesus across the centuries.

A REMARKABLE ACHIEVEMENT

Since this great prayer of Jesus is for the oneness of his followers, in this first point I want to spend some time speaking of the formation of the Uniting Church of Australia in 1977. It's coming about was a remarkable achievement. It took some 50 years of discussion and negotiation from representatives of the Congregational, Methodist and Presbyterian churches to come about. Even then some members of the three Uniting churches didn't come into the Union. Statistics tell us that the Uniting Church is the third largest Christian denomination in Australia behind the Catholic and the Anglican. Each Sunday some 2500 congregations of the Uniting Church come together across Australia. It is the first church to be created in and of Australia. Statistics also tell us that the Uniting church isn't growing which is of course true of a number of churches. There are a number of factors contributing to this but I don't want to spend time looking at them now. It seems that generally churches such as Hill song with a Pentecostal flavour are attracting a number of people at the moment. I do want to highlight a few of what I consider the strengths of the Uniting Church. First of all, it is a Uniting church, most of three previous churches came together which this verse we're considering suggests is what Jesus wanted. Then I consider it is an inclusive church in that there is a broad spectrum of belief within the Christian faith from more conservative in approach to more liberal. Finally, while being concerned about growth in faith for individual members there is a strong emphasis on concern for the total community as shown by the work of Uniting Care and attention to global concerns. So, we have reason to celebrate.

WHAT IS THIS UNITING

According to this verse we're focussing on when defining unity Jesus didn't hold back, he wanted his followers, including us to be one with each other just as he and God, the father are one. This is a very close unity as is set out in the Doctrine of the Trinity, that God is one but known in three persons, father, son and Holy Spirit. I've spent a life time trying to get my head around the doctrine. It implies a unity in which there is no separation. It doesn't seem possible with ordinary human beings. When we consider the way the church has developed through history it seems we've moved further and further away from such unity, starting with the original division between the Catholic and Orthodox churches and then on to the Reformation and the greater and greater number of the denominations within Christianity. When the Uniting Church was under discussion I was in training for the Methodist ministry and during this time the General Conference of the Methodist church in Australia was held in Brisbane. I attended a Session with some of my colleagues in which the coming together of the 3 churches was being discussed. This would have been in about 1956. A prominent Victorian minister whose name, I think was Erwin Voight got up to speak, opposing unity and said, I think being humorous, that he liked his tea and he liked his coffee, but he didn't like to drink them together. He was right that the various denominations have developed their own particular emphases but the central fact is that each one exists to spread the message of Jesus and this provides the unity.

A MAJOR WITNESS

At the end of these verses we're considering, as Jesus prayed that he wanted all those who believed in him to be one with him, he adds. "Then the people of this world will believe that you sent me." At the very least that they will recognise Jesus as warranting the utmost attention and commitment. Instead at the present time we have 100's of denominations. When I was the chaplain at Somerville House, a Uniting and Presbyterian Girl's School in Brisbane, Queensland I took the Year 12 students to visit 5 churches of different denomination as part of Religious Education in a unit called, "Discovering the Church" they were a little mystified in that each of these churches followed the central creeds but had developed different forms of worship and organisation. The same puzzlement exists in the wider community. Christianity is the largest of the world's religions. I hesitate to say that our disunity is the major factor in preventing it becoming larger still as there are a number of factors. I don't believe that there will be any further union between the denominations either in the short or long term. I do believe that these words of Jesus are an appeal and a challenge to constantly seek for togetherness and understanding within our own congregation and to seek co-operation and understanding with other Christian people no matter what they may be called. Amen

QUESTIONS

1. The formation of the Uniting Church of Australia was a remarkable achievement, long in the making. The writer makes the comment towards the end of the sermon that he doesn't consider there is any likelihood of a further coming together

of the churches. Do you agree with the writer, why or why not?

2. Jesus wanted his followers to have the unity he felt with God the Father, a hard unity to define but extremely close. Is such unity an impossible goal? Do you detect any further divisions in the church as a whole? How hard do you find tolerance of different views?

3. What suggestions do you have for greater togetherness and co-operation between Christians of various denominations? What is needed to cultivate tolerance

Acts 2:18 "In those days I will give my spirit to my servants both men and women and they will prophesy."

Prophets All

INTRODUCTION

On the Day of Pentecost in the liturgical calendar we celebrate the event in Jerusalem when the Holy Spirit came upon the disciples. It was, without doubt, the birth of the Christian Church. The flames on the disciples symbolised enthusiasm and the "rushing mighty wind" the winds of change. Until that time the disciples were dispirited and lacking direction. It happened on the day of Pentecost, a Jewish festival 50 days after the festival of the barley sheaf which happened during the Passover. It's for this reason Christians call the coming of the Holy Spirit Pentecost. The charged up Peter spoke to the crowds and quoted the prophet Joel who had been active in about 400 BC. Amongst other things he had said, "In those days . . . He was speaking of a time when the Messiah, God's chosen one would come but I think we're entitled to apply it to those who follow Jesus, as obviously Peter did.

THE BREADTH OF THE PROMISE

When I read these words again and who knows how many times I have done so over the years, it was the phrase, "both men and women will prophesy" which grabbed my attention. Because of the use of the term prophet in connection with the weather and other similar uses, we tend to think of a prophet focussing on predicting the future but the primary function of an ancient prophet was to assess what was going on in the world and using their understanding of what God wanted announce clearly just what they thought that to be, usually introduced by "thus, says the Lord." But both "men and women," this spoken by a Jewish man who as in the days of Jesus would not even speak to his wife in public. One can't prophesy without being rather public. Joel and Peter are very clear in their inclusion of women. There are references throughout the Bible to "prophetesses," Miriam, Moses' sister, Deborah, and about three others and Anna in the Gospels, but the promise in Joel doesn't single out any individuals. Why am I carrying on about this. Because it recognises the place of women who in spite of many individuals being very prominent, have and in many cases still are not treated as, at least, equals.

EVERYONE IS A PROPHET AND A PRIEST

We're speaking about prophets mainly but I've included the title, priest as they tend to go together. When, after Jesus died on the Cross, the veil in the temple, across the Holy of Holies, which could only be entered by the High Priest once a year, tore in two, symbolically the message was that everyone has free access to God and claims to his attention. But Joel indicated everyone would prophesy. I'm going to put this in Christian terms but obviously it was spoken to Jewish people, so everyone who is committed to following Jesus has the ability and opportunity to be aware of what is going on around them, in the church, in their community and nation and from their understanding of the life, attitudes and teaching of Jesus be able to come to a decision of what Jesus would want in that situation and as they have opportunity make that decision known. So, everyone is, in effect, a prophet, a preacher. Obviously, group Bible study and discussion is hugely valuable because we are individuals with different backgrounds. It doesn't mean we have the right to buttonhole people and do the sort of preaching which emphatically announces what we think or preach at people. Also, the most effective preaching is by who we are and how we treat people. Someone wrote, a long time ago, "I can't hear what you're saying because what you are is too loud in my ears.

Prophets All
WHAT ABOUT THE CLERGY?

If everyone is a prophet, preacher and priest where does that leave people like myself, ministers, pastors, priests, vicars and then into the hierarchy moderators, bishops, archbishops, do we still have a role. I hope so but the role of every individual follower of Jesus is just as important. People enter the priesthood, ministry, whatever term is used because they feel called, and there will be a story behind each one, my own story is in line with what someone has called "open and shut doors," one course slamming in one's face and another door opening. I believe as long as there are churches there will be a place for ministers who are almost always full time, and therefore able to devote more time to the challenges and responsibilities of a church, to work with a congregation and seek to bring care, guidance, hopefully insights. Many churches are struggling but I believe firmly still have an important place in the community and world, to provide fellowship, support but above all to hold before people the person, attitudes and teaching of Jesus and to demonstrate the positive effects following him has. Each time we gather in the church we have the opportunity for recommitment and to find fresh incentive. Amen

QUESTIONS

1. In most Christian denominations, but not all, women are able to be ministers or clergy, whatever title you are familiar with. What is your attitude to this long overdue development; the overdue being particularly sparked by the quotes in the first point? Is there opportunity for further advancement in your denomination?
2. In my early experiences in the church, through the Methodist variety, there was an emphasis on offering for "full time service," in other words, to be people whose sole occupation is work for the church in some role. In what sense can every

individual follower of Jesus, whatever their occupation be a prophet as defined in point 2.

3. People do not seem at this time in 2024 to be flocking to offer for the ministry. Can you suggest reasons for this shortage? What sort of job description would you write for a well-functioning, modern minister?

Romans 6:15 "Does it mean that we are free to sin because we are ruled by God's wonderful kindness and not by law"
NEB "Are we free to sin because we are not under the law but under grace"

A Vital Balance

INTRODUCTION

Someone has pointed out that in most of his other letters Paul had already visited the places and people to whom he wrote but in the case of the letter to the Romans he had not yet visited Rome and certainly would not have imagined he would get there is chains. This letter introduces Paul's approach to the faith he was proclaiming.

THE TRADITION OF PAUL

Paul's letters have had a huge influence on Christian doctrine and on the spread of Christianity. Wilson, a naturalist who was with Scott in the Antarctic once wrote in regard to Paul, "Dear good old saint, we gentiles thank you." He was right, it is doubtful if the message would have got beyond the Jews if Saul had not had his vision on the road to Damascus. Saul who became known as Paul after that experience had been, as he wrote, a Pharisee of the Pharisees. The Pharisees were an extremely devout sect within Judaism who lived by the law, not just the 10 commandments but rigid detailed requirements spelling out how every detail of life should be carried out. For example, the law which said that people should not work on the Sabbath meant even that a tailor should not leave a needle in his clothing as that would be bearing a burden. When Paul said he was a Pharisee of the Pharisees he meant that he surpassed others in the carrying out of the various requirements. When the early disciples started to preach and teach about Jesus, Saul, the Pharisee thought they threatened Judaism, Jews would move away from their religion. He started persecuting Christians and was present when Stephen, an early deacon was stoned to death. The way Stephen died asking for forgiveness for those killing him had a large effect on Paul. He was on the road to Damascus to try to get rid of more of the pesky Christians when he had a blinding vision of Jesus. Eventually, out of his legalism and his efforts to stamp out the early Christian faith came his belief that an individual does not get into favour with God, be accepted and lead a worthwhile life by what they do in obeying various rules but by being dependent on God in Jesus and allowing God to work in one's life. It was this understanding which fired Paul's desire to spread the message of Christianity and which at other points in the History of the church had a particular influence on other key figures. I'll mention just two. In the 16th century Luther came to understand this doctrine and was instrumental in the Reformation. Much later John and Charles Wesley were part of a group of Christians whose attention to discipline and a highly regulated life led to them being nicknamed Methodists. One night John Wesley attended a meeting when someone was reading an Introduction to Paul's letter to the Romans. He had a life changing experience and wrote, "I felt I did trust in Christ, Christ alone for salvation and an assurance was given me . . ."

BECOMING A FOLLOWER OF JESUS

I felt I needed to give that rather lengthy review to lead to closer attention to our text. "Are we to sin because we are not under law but under grace." Obviously, some of the Christians in Rome had taken Paul's emphasis on grace too seriously, feeling they didn't need to live good lives by following basic rules, rather, they, having made a response of faith to God had it made, so to speak. I grew up in a Methodist church and the church was my life. Much of the preaching I heard in Church services, Youth camps and various rallies put before me, not only being committed to Jesus and accepting the benefits of his life and death but having the assurance of being accepted. This led to a rather constant search for this experience which proved to be elusive. It wasn't until my second burst of study in America that I came to the understanding that this wasn't for me but rather a willingness to be committed to Jesus and his way of life, no matter how I felt. There is more than one way of becoming a follower of Jesus. It is a process of working towards likeness to Jesus. How successful one is, according to Jesus is judged by our attitude to others, particularly those in need.

THE VITAL BALANCE

I feel that the words of our text indicate that Paul was realising that his emphasis on God's grace and its free nature needed to be balanced by a following of positive directions. He did this in some magnificent passages such as 1 Corinthians 13 where he defined love. Years ago, I remember in some sermons, in an effort to promote the place of grace preachers speaking of the boast of certain people, "I'm a self-made man." Of course, there has never been such a person, for a start any individual needs the coming together of the genes of their parents to have life, then there is all that contributes to the people we are, people such as siblings, friends, people in the community who work to provide our needs, teachers, authors, entertainment figures. We need grace, we need acceptance, therefore thankfulness is an essential characteristic for each of us but we need commitment to a way of life and for us this is found in Jesus and the church which exists to promote and assist this. Amen

QUESTIONS

1. One of Jesus's last words to his disciples was to go into the world and make people his disciples. Paul really ventured out to people other than his own. There seems to have been in recent years a renewed emphasis on discipleship, how do you

see yourself carrying out the challenge of Jesus and what are the difficulties in this age?

2. How did you become a follower of Jesus, if you accept that description of yourself? Do you recognise different ways people may have of becoming followers of Jesus?

3. Erich Fromm, psychiatrist, suggested that becoming independent was the mark of adulthood. Do you think Paul's words in this text aid one's sense of independence?

Romans 12:5 "There are many of us, but we are each part of the body of Christ, as well as part of one another."

Jesus's People

INTRODUCTION

We can thank Paul, the apostle that we are meeting together for worship here as part of the church universal. When Saul, the Pharisee, in other words one of the strictest sects of the Jews at the time of Jesus, had his transforming experience on the way to Jerusalem from Damascus he undertook the role of seeking to include non-Jews in the ongoing movement which became known as Christianity. In the verse we're focussing on he referred to the church as the body of Christ. In one phrase he set out the major reason for existence of the church.

THE CHURCH AS THE BODY OF CHRIST

So what can we take from those few words. This is written some 1990 years after the death of Jesus. Jesus lived for 33 brief years from the start of what has become known as the "common era" but we are in "the year of our Lord" 2024. In those 33 years, really in about 3 years, Jesus built on the teachings of the great people of faith of his people the Jews who had preceded him. In some cases, he re-interpreted those teachings, in some cases he gave fresh insights and ways of understanding. All the time he proclaimed the presence in the world of the Kingdom or rule of God. In a nutshell what he was doing in those brief 3 years was setting out in his teaching and attitudes the way God wanted people to live, in other words, getting the most out of life while giving the most to it. The people of his day could see him, hear him and if they could overcome their reverence, feel him. We in the church who like the disciples seek to follow him, for that is what the church is all about, have the responsibility and privilege of representing him in the world. Towards the end of his 3-year ministry, some Greek people came to Philip one of the disciples and asked to see Jesus. It is the major role of the church and each one who is a part of it to seek to show the effects of following Jesus and to proclaim in every way possible the vision Jesus had and has for the world.

EACH ONE OF US HAS A PLACE IN THE CHURCH

As has already been indicated Paul in this verse speaks of the church as the body of Christ. In a few places in his writings, he mentions that the body has many parts and so does the church. We are all part of the body of Christ of which he is the head. We know more and more about the brain but still have a lot to learn. We do know that the brain is the source of ideas and sparks movement and we could go on and on. So, to be a sincere and worthwhile part of the church we each need to have responded or to respond to a similar challenge to that experienced by the first disciples- follow me. In other words, learn from me, what I taught, the attitudes I had, the concerns I have. Of course, each of us has our own background, family, schooling, interests, occupation but when it comes to our attitudes, we are challenged to translate the attitudes Jesus had into each situation, compassion, concern, patience, tolerance. Whatever congregation of the church we are in we each bring our particular skills, aptitudes and interest to further that particular part of the church.

OUR LINKAGE

Paul made a very telling extension of his statement that each person in the church is a part of the body of Christ when he wrote, "as well as part of one another." Paul spoke a mouthful right there, to be a part of the church whichever it might be is to be linked to one another. I believe this thought of Paul's, having grown up in the church and experienced the fellowship of a great number of churches including while living in three different countries. When we follow Jesus within the church, we become part of a caring, concerned community. But that doesn't just happen. When Paul wrote to the church in Colossae he wrote to a congregation having trouble getting on together. In Colossians 3:12 he set out some of the attitudes they needed to adopt, to be gentle, kind, humble, meek, patient. The next part is translated differently in different versions, to be tolerant, forbearing and the most blunt is in the version I mostly use, "the Bible for Today," "Put up with one another." The thing is that we may all be seeking to follow Jesus but we are all different and it is a massive challenge to love one another. It is utterly impossible to like everyone but we can respect one another and be tolerant. Finally, I want to extend this final thought of Paul's in the verse we're considering almost infinitely. Scientists tells us that every human being is genetically linked and in a blow to the white supremacists the linkage goes back to Africa. The point is we are all human beings so we need to at least "put up with one another" The second commandment is "to love people as ourselves." Amen.

QUESTIONS

1. No matter how large or small an individual church is, the description of Paul the apostle, it is "the body of Christ" applies. In this day and age when the church is mostly struggling, how can churches best be the "body of Christ" and represent him to the world at large?

2. There have been many suggestions throughout the centuries as to how the church in any age can be directed by Jesus. Here are a few and you may be able to add others a. Establish a hierarchy, Pope, Cardinals, Arch Bishops, Bishops, Priests. All denominations have different titles but the above is a sample.

b. Pray, Christians have met for prayer throughout the ages and asked what Jesus would want them to do. Usually, the answer is accepted by consensus. c. Some individual feels inspired enough and confident enough to persuade a number of others they have the answer. d. People consider deeply the teaching and attitudes of Jesus and choose a course of action which lines up most truly with what they have learned. Which of these or additional responses do you consider are most acceptable?

3. There was a saying which has come down from the first couple of centuries A.D. when Christians were suffering terrible persecution and supported one another as they went to their deaths, "see how these Christians love one another." That saying has been used at times in mockery when disputes are going on in the church. The church can and does provide acceptance, support, fellowship to people of various ages, sexes, races, classes. Have you seen this happen and how was it worked out?

Romans 12:21 "Don't let evil defeat you but defeat evil with good"

Be Good

INTRODUCTION

Sometimes when we're leaving a place we will hear the words, "Be good." If we hear those words as an adult, they will usually be uttered by someone as somewhat of a joke. Paul wrote about being good in his letter to the Romans. It's a word which is used a great deal in many contexts in English. If we ask someone how they are they will often say, "I'm good thanks." If it's someone I know well I will sometimes say you mean well. I looked up the meaning of good in our pocket Macquarie Dictionary and in just this concise form I found 17 ways of using it from, "morally excellent, righteous, pious" to a "greeting or farewell" as in "good afternoon" or "goodnight." Of course, we are using it in the first sense I mentioned.

ROLE MODELS

We come into the world as babies with no sense of what is wanted or expected and react with content if something happens, we're comfortable with like warmth, or a pleasant face or express our dislike of something which brings discomfort like feeling hungry or having a wet nappy. It becomes a fairly rapid learning process. As we grow, we learn what behaviours are acceptable and those which are not. Hopefully we'll be reproved when we do or say something which is hurtful to others and be commended when we do something which helps us to fit happily into the family or community.

BE GOOD

We are fortunate if people such as parents, siblings and community figures not only tell us what is acceptable or unacceptable but more times than not model what is acceptable. Learning right from wrong is most successful if we have good role models. I've always found it amazing how the reactions my parents showed have very often come to the fore when dealing with our own children perhaps when having to use discipline. We are fortunate indeed that in the gospels we have a record of the teaching and attitudes of Jesus as an example of how best to live. It's interesting that on one occasion a rich young man came to Jesus and asked "Teacher, what good thing must I do to have eternal life?" Jesus replied, "Why do you ask me about what is good? Only God is good. If you want to have eternal life, you must obey the commandments." The young man asked which commandments he should obey and Jesus replied, "Do not murder. Be faithful in marriage, do not steal. Do not tell lies about others. Respect your father and mother. And love others as much as you love yourself." (Matthew 19:17–19) In his reply Jesus doesn't even claim to be good but I don't think anyone could find a better model of goodness.

PAUL'S DEFINITION

In his answer to the young man Jesus quoted the second commandment on love, "love others as much as you love yourself." Paul spelt out what the sort of love spoken about by Jesus really involves in his letter to the people in the church in Corinth and I don't think there's a better definition of how to live a good life so we'll look at it in some detail. It's in first Corinthians 13:4–8. It will not be the only time in these sermons this passage is mentioned, I believe it spells out in clear fashion part of what it means to follow Jesus. As we go through these words of Paul the most striking thing, is that they are so basic. Since we are individuals some of these attitudes will be more natural for us than others. It is important that we know ourselves. During my second big bout of study in America when I worked part time as a cleaner, for some of the time I worked for a feller who at one stage decided to do poker work, burning

Be Good

words or scenes into wood with a hot iron. He gave me one of his early attempts with the words, "Noel thyself" on it. We don't have time to look in detail at what Paul suggests "love is kind and patient," kind, being considerate, having others well-being at heart; patient- being accepting and ready to wait, "never jealous." I guess accepting what one is and has, "never boastful, proud or rude," rudeness can easily develop when one takes another for granted, "isn't selfish," one of the most difficult attitudes to keep in check, or "quick tempered" certainly a characteristic which varies from person to person and maybe could be a greater problem as one ages, "doesn't keep a record of wrongs," "being ready to forgive" dealing with issues as they occur, "rejoices in the truth but not in evil"—finding no pleasure in what is wrong "being ready to face the truth" and then back to the positive, "always supportive, loyal," essential in a long term relationship, "trusting," being open and accepting. It's a high standard but one we can aspire to and forgiveness is available readily and there needs to be a readiness to seek it with others as well as God.

A REAL TEST

The last part of this passage deals with taking revenge. It starts with the words, "don't try to get even" and ends with the words of our text, "Don't let evil defeat you but defeat evil with good." The desire to get even is a natural reaction and is condoned in some religions but not in Christianity. Matthew records Jesus saying, "You know that you have been taught, "An eye for an eye and a tooth for a tooth." But I tell you not to try to get even with a person who has done something to you. When someone slaps your right cheek, turn and let that person slap your other cheek." (Matthew 5:38) Paul quotes some words from Proverbs, "If your enemies are hungry give them something to eat. And if they are thirsty give them something to drink. This will be the same as piling burning coals on their heads." Which I think means this action will be so unexpected that they may be ashamed. Difficult as it may be to avoid seeking to get even to do so stops a nasty situation from developing and means that one can go on with the rest of life without being consumed by the thought of revenge.

I want to conclude with a quote from John Wesley which is a major challenge, as with the Corinthian passage this quote from Wesley will occur again in these sermons.

"Do all the good you can, by all the means you can, in all the ways you can, in all the places you can, at all the times you can, to all the people you can, as long as ever you can."

QUESTIONS

1. There was a time in my training for the ministry when speaking of Jesus as an example was frowned on. The implication being he was far more than that. How important to you are the actions and attitudes of Jesus as recounted in the gospels?

2. Who have been the major role models in your life? Why is that the case?

3. Are there any of the attributes of love Paul mentions which are more important to you than others? Which are the most difficult for you to live up to?

4. Jesus turned the "eye for an eye" teaching of Judaism on its head in the passage mentioned in point 3. Do you find it difficult not to bear grudges? If you are considering this in a group you may find this difficult to answer. If you feel that you cannot free yourself from a particular grudge you may need to seek help.

1 **Corinthians 1: 23** "But we preach that Christ was nailed to a cross. Most Jews have problems with this, most gentiles think it foolish."

Jesus Crucified

INTRODUCTION

A cross has become the symbol of Christianity and of course it features prominently in many churches and is often worn as a pendant.

THE CROSS

With a cross becoming the symbol of Christianity there may be times when we forget that when Jesus lived crosses were very common sights for people of the day. Crucifixion was the method of capital punishment chosen by the Romans. History tells us that on one occasion after a revolt of slaves 2000 were crucified and lined a roadway. I chose not to watch Mel Gibson's movie, "The Passion of Christ" as I had seen reviews which told of its realistically depicted scenes. I was first confronted by what crucifixion involved at an Easter camp at Currumbin, when one of the exercises was putting together a newspaper about the events of Easter. I was in a group which was tasked to do some research on crucifixion. We mainly consulted a book by Jim Bishop, "The Day Christ Died." Crucifixion is one of the most horrendous forms of capital punishment devised by human kind. Again, incidentally I am a long-time opponent of capital punishment. The details of crucifixion make terrible reading. In spite of artistic representations of wounds in the hands, the nails were driven through the wrists as otherwise the nails could not support the weight of the person being crucified. The weight of the person dragging down meant that they had great trouble breathing and they would endeavour to force themselves up until eventually exhaustion made that impossible. It is not a pleasant account but I'm sharing it as many times I feel that what Jesus went through is romanticised.

VIEWS OF THE CROSS

Paul stresses that he preached about Jesus being crucified. Really, this is the only incident about the life of Jesus which found its way into the History of the day, other than the Gospels. Paul commented that there were differing views of the significance of the crucifixion. "Most Jews" he suggested had problems with it. The problems arose because for centuries the Jews had awaited a Messiah, a Christ, God's chosen one who would restore the nation to the prominence it had under David, the King, and rescue them from oppression. When Jesus was moving around teaching, they were always asking him for a sign, to engineer some spectacular event. Crucifixion fell a long way short of what they expected. Non-Jews, Gentiles, Paul wrote thought the crucifixion of Jesus to be foolish. They thought it was foolish because the early followers of Jesus were suggesting that Jesus was divine, he was more than man, he was a god. In their eyes the suggestion that someone who could be a god, could be subjected to such an horrific death was ridiculous. The traditional Christian view of Jesus being crucified is that it was instrumental in human beings having the possibility of forgiveness. I want to suggest another possible view. When Jesus went through his time in a desert region after his baptism when I believe he sorted out how he was going to go about his ministry, one of the possibilities was to use evil, forceful ways to gain control of the kingdoms of the world. Jesus rejected that idea. He went about his ministry with kindness, compassion and concern in the hopes that people would respond, as of course, many did. He espoused non-violence. In the course of that approach, he went to the cross. The cross, I believe, became a symbol of what must be the approach of anyone who would follow Jesus, non-violence. Sadly, given the fact that some individuals or groups seek to gain control of others by violent means then violent resistance becomes necessary.

BEARING THE CROSS

Jesus made sure that the cross and its significance became a part of the life of his followers when he said, "You must take up your cross and follow me." You'll see I called this point, "Bearing the Cross." It made me think of a joke I heard many, many years ago. I'm not sure I ever sang the hymn which is mentioned. Apparently, a little girl was once asked why she had called her teddy bear, "gladly." She said that since the bear's eyes were a little crooked, it reminded her of the hymn she sang in Sunday School which went, "gladly my cross I'd bear." There's been a lot of discussion over the years as to what Jesus meant when he said "take up your cross." Some have suggested he meant all his followers would have particular difficulties and challenges to face eg a handicap of some kind, or a particular loss and we need to deal with those difficulties and not be overcome by them. There is truth there but I want to suggest that he meant that if we're sincere in our following we need to adopt the attitudes of compassion and active concern which he had. We can't allow ourselves to be complacent and withdraw ourselves from concern. This is one of the prime values of our prayers of intercession when we think of people who are being oppressed or respond to appeals for support for those in need or sign an appeal for release from unjust imprisonment through Amnesty International. It's a great time to consider how we view the cross and above all respond to the challenge of Jesus, "You must take up your cross and follow him." Years ago, a man attending the Oberamegau passion play at the end of the play approached the man, Anton Lang, who had played the part of Jesus, and asked if he could have his photo taken with the cross used in the play on his shoulder. When Anton Lang put the cross on the man's shoulder, he staggered and nearly fell. He said I had no idea the cross was real. Anton Lang replied, "Unless I feel the weight of the cross, I cannot play my part." Amen

QUESTIONS

1. Do you think the crucifixion has been romanticised as in the hymn, "the old rugged cross"? Do you feel that is helpful?
2. Should anyone who is a follower of Jesus be a supporter of capital punishment?
3. The second point elaborates on what Paul wrote about the Jewish and Greek view of the cross. For most Christians Jesus going to the cross is necessary to God granting forgiveness for sin, "atonement." Do you think the idea is credible?
4. The teaching and attitudes of Jesus suggest that if one wants to follow his way, serving other people, other forms of life and the earth is inescapable. What forms of service are you involved in?

Galatians 5: 13-14—My friends, you were chosen to be free. So don't use your freedom as an excuse to do anything you want. Use it as an opportunity to serve each other with love. All that the law says can be summed up in the command to love others as much as you love yourself.

The Essential Guide to Worthwhile Living

INTRODUCTION

There can be no doubt that Paul the apostle largely shaped Christian doctrine so that I have come to wonder over the years if his thought clouded what is essential Christian belief, but passages like the one we're considering this morning remind me that he was both feisty and down to earth.

GUIDED AND THOUGHTFUL FREEDOM

Paul reminded the Galatians and reminds us that genuine Christian faith is freeing. Even though he was writing to a predominantly non Jewish community he always in his ministry started with the Jews who happened to be in each place or who had embraced the Jewish faith. When these people decided to become Christians one of the big pluses would have been the relief from not having to be involved in the constant detail of the law—so a real sense of freedom. However, it is a sense of freedom which is offered to anyone who is committed to Jesus and his way of life. Freedom from guilt—from lack of purpose—from lack of direction. Jesus was life affirming, people affirming, earth affirming as John records him as saying, "I came so that everyone would have life, and have it in its fullest." There's a saying which was used occasionally some years ago, "Get a life" usually spoken to someone who is bogged down in some activity which is utterly time consuming and doesn't seem to be going anywhere. I think Jesus would have adopted it. Paul goes a step further to seek to correct a misinterpretation by some of the Galatian church who felt that having received freedom as Christians they could now do what they liked without consideration for others. It certainly was and would always be a mistaken idea. Paul took this thought a step further in his next statement.

THE CRUCIAL COMMANDMENT

So Paul wrote—"All that the law says can be summed up in the command to love others as much as you love yourself." It's interesting to remember that Paul never actually met Jesus even though he did meet those who had done so, Peter, John and James, the brother of Jesus. He does, of course, speak of meeting Jesus in a visionary sense. This insight of Paul's ties in with the response Jesus made to someone who wanted to know which was the greatest commandment? Jesus replied that the greatest was to "love God with heart soul mind and strength and equal to it was this commandment which Paul mentioned. Even before Jesus quoted these commandments they had a very long tradition for they were and are part of the Jewish scriptures which we call the Old Testament. If one examines the 10 commandments which have for a long, long time been regarded as a guide to worthwhile living, it is possible to see that Paul is spot on in saying that the command to love others does sum up the 10. The first of the ten sets out the need to love God but the rest, other than the one dealing with the observation of the Sabbath directly speak of how one is to treat others. This is an essential guide to living. The word used for love here and wherever the commandment is quoted does not mean romantic love but rather a strong and constant concern and respect for other people. When in doubt as to a course of action we should take it is a good exercise and many times a difficult one to ask, "what is the loving thing to do." The degree to which we love others is set in the words, "as we love ourselves."

WHAT IS A CHRISTIAN?

In the light of these words of Paul it seems in point to ask, "what is a Christian?" I guess in this I'm sharing one of my own struggles but I know I'm not alone. I grew up in an evangelical tradition, to be specific in the Methodist church at Graceville. A great deal of preaching and teaching had to do with salvation, assurance and sanctification and therefore the idea that Christian belief made a difference and the sense that one had the assurance of being accepted. I had a great deal of trouble coming to terms with the fact, and this was over a great many years that there were people outside the church who made no claims to being Christian whose lives in terms of compassion and active concern for others were a rebuke to me. So what was this difference that from all accounts had been made in me because I was very sincere in my belief and commitment. I think the point is to be ready to accept people as they are and rejoice in positive attitudes we see. Also I am happy to be the person I am, with all the contributions that have shaped me through my family and a life time of involvement in the church. As we have opportunity I feel we should be ready to share what following Jesus has meant to us. Paul, in a later verse in this chapter writes of the fruit of the spirit which is an imposing list being, "happy, peaceful, patient, kind, good faithful and self-controlled." These are the characteristics which can grow in someone who has oriented their life in the way Jesus spelt out. We're on a journey and the learning process never stops. It's good from time to time to ask ourselves how we're going. The great thing about the church is the feeling that can be ever present that we are on this journey together and that we are here for mutual support and encouragement.

QUESTIONS

1. Have you had an experience of being weighed down by events in your life or decisions you have made? If you currently have a sense of freedom or ease, what brought that sense about?

2. How well do you think you are observing the commandment to love others as much as your love yourself? Is there a limit to your concern and respect governed by race, nation or sex? How thorough is your sense of self-esteem?

3. There have been moves in recent years to look for the positives in all religions such as compassion as a way to greater world harmony. Do you think such moves could be fruitful?

Afterword
The Art of Preaching

Preaching and its fruit, the sermon, have many times developed a bad press and become the butt, many times, of appropriate jokes. The sometimes applicability of the jokes will hopefully become plain in what follows.

One of the most unexpected down putting of preaching came from no less than the Apostle Paul in his first letter to the church at Corinth. In the early translations of the Bible, in that particular letter, Paul referred to "the foolishness of preaching." (1 Corinthians 1:21) Later translations make plain that Paul, in that part of his letter, was drawing attention to the fact that aspects of the message of Christianity appeared foolish to both Jews and Greeks. However the traditional place or role of preaching and the sermon in some parts of society are still a mystery to many.

Preaching has, over the centuries been a major instrument in bringing about the spread of Christianity and I suspect to some extent Islam. Since my background in upbringing and training for the ministry is Methodist I am most familiar with the impact which the preaching of John Wesley had in the movement which brought about a revival in the church in England at that time. The accounts of Wesley's epic journeys around England on horseback preaching from place to place tell of crowds mounting to the hundreds gathering to listen to him and be deeply affected. This is a fact of History but I have to admit that it has always filled me with wonder. One of the requirements for admission to training

Afterword

for the Methodist ministry was to attest that one had read a book entitled, "Wesley's 44 Sermons." I'm sure he preached more than 44 but someone obviously made a selection. I struggled through these rather voluminous sermons, full of abstruse doctrine, so I could with some honesty attest I had read them. At the same time I wondered how people without a great deal of education could understand them and even more remarkably be brought to new faith by them, but apparently they did.

On one of our trips which took in the British Isles my wife, Mary and I found our way to Bristol where we came across Wesley's church which has a statue of him on horseback in front. We discovered that John Wesley often stayed there. There was a gallery and the story was that when someone was in training to be a preacher and was engaged in leading a church service Wesley would walk around the gallery. This would enable him to look at the preacher's presentation and from a different view point, the response of the congregation. In other words he was convinced of the place of preaching in the ongoing life of the church. I flatter myself in thinking that this practice of Wesley's indicates that he would endorse the title of this afterword, "The Art of Preaching."

My observations of ministerial training in the U.S.A. and here in Queensland have suggested that training in preaching may not be given the emphasis it received in rather earlier decades when I trained for the Methodist ministry. It seems that in most cases "preaching" is an optional subject in the involved courses whereas in the training I'm familiar with "preaching class" was mandatory. Many aspects of what follows in relation to the sermon and preaching have come from my experience of preaching class which I think will be valuable for me to describe. Each year of our training for ministry we were expected to prepare a complete church service and then conduct it before the Master and Deputy Master of the College and all our colleagues. Each of the students was allotted an aspect of the church service to criticise, such as for the sermon, exegesis and homiletics and for the service itself, choice of hymns, prayers etc. Most of those training for ministry at the time, including myself, had spent some time before

College as Probationers or Home Missionaries so had preached regularly. For my first appearance I selected a sermon and service which had received favourable comments from at least some of the congregation who had attended. As, at that time, most candidates for the ministry were rather young, congregations generally were encouraging. At the critique to follow the service the comments were mostly critical with some reaching scathing. The particular sermon never again saw the light of day. In other words some tough but necessary lessons were learned and one was launched on developing the art of preaching.

THE SERMON

As I stated earlier in the Preface the sermons in this book and this afterword on "The Art of Preaching" are based on verses or passages of the Bible. Around the turn of the 19th to 20th century, some preachers such as Dr Lesley Weatherhead based at least some sermons on passages from philosophy or literature. At times people still preach topical sermons such as, perhaps, "Dealing with Suffering." For the purposes of this afterword the sermon is based on "Scripture."

CHOOSING A TEXT

For the uninitiated, a text is the verse or passage from the Bible on which a sermon is based. This is most times a verse which for whatever reason, experience maybe or circumstances, attracts the attention of the preacher. Early in my preaching, given my Methodist background, the choice of text would be regarded as God's leading and would most times come from a part of the Bible one was studying at the time, a personally favourite passage, or responding to particular circumstances. When the Uniting Church came about with the union of most of the members of the Congregational, Methodist and Presbyterian Churches, the church joined with the Catholic, Anglican and Lutheran churches in following a

Afterword

lectionary of readings for a church's year. I have always applauded the decision in that the choice of passages or verses on which to base a sermon was narrowed. Each Sunday there is a suggested passage from the early books of the Bible and the prophets, a Psalm, a reading from the Acts of the Apostles or one of the various Letters and the Gospels. I found this particularly valuable in the last 11 years of my ministry when I was Chaplain in a Church school. Part of my role was to lead brief devotions in Assemblies, Chapel services for the various Year levels, at the time Years 8–12 and Boarder's services. Each year I purchased the Anglican lectionary in addition to the Uniting Church version as it has readings for every day of the year. I consider that this focussed choice helped preserve my sanity. Another value of following a lectionary is that it encourages a wider choice of text, beyond ones favourites.

CHOOSING A THEME

I believe it's extremely valuable both for a preacher and a congregation for each sermon and indeed church service to have a theme. I hadn't followed this practice, again, until the Uniting Church came about and I noticed the mention of "theme" in one of the early services prepared for Holy Communion. Having a theme provides a degree of unity to a sermon and can do the same if followed for the whole of a church service.

SERMON AND SERVICE PREPARATION

Quite often over the years, usually friendly jokes, have been made about a minister only working one day a week. The person joking in this fashion is most times unaware of the pastoral and organisational work of a minister. They may not, however, be aware of the amount of time needed to prepare a service and a sermon. Different people will need differing time periods and I have to say that the longer one lives and has a variety of experiences, the easier it becomes, but I believe a rough estimate of preparation time would be 5 hours. After deciding on a text and theme my own practice is to then, decide on the sermon points. I like to do all that without consulting a commentary, that is, a book written about the particular book of the Bible including explanatory comments about the verse or passage being used in the sermon. Having spoken of commentaries in book form I am aware that in 2024 when I am writing this there are almost endless resources on line. I believe it is extremely important to work out the direction one plans on taking in dealing with a particular verse and theme. Quite apart from avoiding plagiarism, one's own slant on a verse or theme could be especially helpful to some in a congregation. I personally choose a text and theme, if possible, a couple of weeks before the actual preparation as the mind seems to keep working on it, without one necessarily being aware of it.

EXEGESIS

This exercise involves placing the selected verse or passage in context, that is, how it fits into the account from which it has been taken. The value of this process is mainly that it ensures that the overall intention of the speaker or writer is more likely to be made clear making it more difficult for the preacher to follow out his personal whim.

HOMILETICS—HOMILETICS IS THE STRUCTURE OF THE SERMON.

The main consideration is the use of points so that the various aspects of the message can be made more plain. The process will be well illustrated in the sermons in this book. The number of points used by a preacher will vary in accord with the passage being considered and the practice of the particular preacher. Personally, almost without exception I choose to use three points. Partly this has been brought about by an experience early in my preparation for ministry. At the time, it was necessary to submit a written sermon

AFTERWORD

to Synod and Conference as well as conducting a service. This process occurred both as a candidate for ministerial training and in each of the six years of training. In my year at Home Missionary Training College, I was introduced to a book to do with preaching. The writer suggested that when preparing a sermon, one should have main points and that these should be divided into headings and the headings into sub-headings. When I submitted my written sermon to Synod as a Candidate I followed this suggested process I heard that the person reading it called it a "many headed hydra." These days when most churches have a data projector it is possible to have the headings of the points on the screen. When the use of Power Point came into effect I included a summary of the message at each point but discovered that it was rather a distraction. As in every presentation, spoken or written, it is important to have an introduction which may contain background to verse or passage or a short statement on the theme designed to capture the attention of the congregation. Also, after the points have been expounded there should be a conclusion, a summary perhaps or a challenge emphasising the theme.

ILLUSTRATIONS

It was tempting to head this section, "the art of illustrating" as there are some preachers who excel in choice of illustrations. By this I mean stories or quotes either from one's personal experiences, or from what one has read which shed further light on the points being made. Jesus was an absolute master at this practice. He made regular use of "parables," stories with a punch line, to illustrate his message. For these he drew on his observation of practices involved in the household, the farm or fishing. The illustrations need, of course, to be appropriate. When one restricts a sermon to 10 minutes I've discovered that overuse of illustrations may occupy too much time and therefore restrict getting the message across.

PREACHING

The Setting

In most cases a preacher has to use the area available in a church from which to conduct a service. There will be at least a raised area so that the preacher is visible to the congregation and vice versa. There could well also be a pulpit of varying height. The highest pulpit I have ever experienced was in a church in Melbourne. It's only a slight exaggeration to suggest that one began to worry about a possible snowfall. More recent churches mostly just have a platform with a lectern so that the preacher can move around, more about that later. Personally where possible I like to be able to move a lectern closer to a congregation so that one is not too far removed from them.

To Move or Not

A recent tendency is for preachers to move around a platform while preaching, of course, only possible when there is no pulpit. Following this procedure is up to the whim of a particular preacher and perhaps on the expectation of the congregation. Personally when listening to a "perambulating" preacher I find it rather distracting. Obviously in my own preaching I remain in a pulpit or behind a lectern.

Use of Voice

I started preaching before churches had speaker systems so that one needed to project the voice and preaching up to 4 times a Sunday was a strain. Today that is not a problem but endeavouring to speak clearly is absolutely necessary and to modulate the voice so as to avoid a sleep producing drone. My memory for jokes is not good but I remember hearing of one preacher who used notes, who one Sunday left his notes in the pulpit and they were read by a member of the congregation. At one point, in the margin, he had written in big letters, "Shout like hell here, argument weak." Preachers shouting in their presentation should be a sometimes practice, used for emphasis and with sincerity. Excessive use becomes wearing for any congregation.

Early in my training for the ministry I read my first book to do with Psychology of Religion. It was written by Robert H. Thouless and was titled just that. In one section he spoke about the emphasis in some services on an evangelical appeal, that is, asking people, at the end of a challenging sermon to come to the front of the church as an indication of their readiness to be committed to Jesus. He mentioned, in particular, the use of hymns which made a lot of use of "come" and "coming," and of course, the same usage in the actual sermon. It drew my attention to the possibility of services and sermons being oriented towards certain outcomes. I'm including this statement as I believe, very often, excessive shouting, gesturing, pacing a platform are designed to push people to a response. I don't think I'm alone in finding that such practices are indeed off putting. I believe that a preacher should endeavour to shape her/his message so that people have the opportunity to think along with what is being presented and to arrive at their own conclusion.

Use of Notes

Very few speakers of any description are able to speak without referring to notes. What can vary is the degree one needs to be dependent on one's notes. I've known preachers who show a degree of pride in being able to dispense with notes. Personally I feel more confident in preaching with the use of notes no matter how familiar I am with a particular sermon. It is, however, highly recommended to work at reducing one's dependence on notes as it is essential in preaching for the congregation to see one's eyes and vice versa. I have memories in the early days of my training of a minister who adopted an unusual stance when preaching, he bent over backwards so that a congregation was never aware he was looking at them. When he was questioned about the practice he said that in

England when he preached it was most times in churches with galleries and he was told that a preacher should keep running their eyes along the gallery so both people in the gallery and those in the body of the church would feel they were being looked at. The practice certainly didn't work in the average church in Australia. Reading one's sermon is, I believe, a definite no –no, unless one can do so looking up very frequently as one loses touch with the congregation. I heard about a minister who had become dependent on extensive notes. One Sunday he decided to preach on the Garden of Eden. He got to the part of the account when Adam and Eve realised they were naked, as he turned a page there was a lengthy pause as he frantically looked around. Over the speaker system the congregation heard, "there seems to be a leaf missing."

Use of Gestures

In most forms of public speaking the use of gestures is important. The usage is more natural to some than others. Overuse, I believe, can be off putting but if they seem natural they can emphasise and even aid the points being made. In our training for the ministry at King's College the administration, in their wisdom arranged for students to have at least one session with an actor, Harry Borridale. He worked on enunciation and use of gestures. I have to confess that after my first preaching class it was recommended that I have extra sessions with him. I think he did help with the enunciation but I'm not so sure about the gestures. I have strong memories of him saying that good gestures start from the side of the body, the arm moves up towards the front and then out to the side. To me, at the time, it all seemed too structured and unnatural. I do use gestures when I'm preaching which must appear natural as on one occasion after taking a number of services at a particular church, a lady commented about the use of my hands. Such favourable comments are nothing if not encouraging.

Afterword

Avoidance of Mannerisms

This may seem a little pedantic but it's included for the sake of avoiding distractions from the message. Over the many years I have listened to various preachers. I have encountered one minister, some time ago, who made frequent use of "brethren" when addressing the congregation. My sister and I engaged in keeping a count. He also on occasion slapped the pulpit for emphasis which did get one's attention. Another had adopted a mannerism of blinking rapidly until he made a point when his eyes opened quite wide. There was another who frequently looked off to the side. As in any habit if one becomes conscious of some quirk developing the sooner, having become aware, one gets it under control the better. It is helpful to have a spouse or partner or congregation member to draw one's attention to whatever the mannerism is.

Dealing with Nervousness

When one is speaking in public it is almost inevitable that one will be nervous. A well-known preacher was once asked if he became nervous before preaching. He answered that the day he didn't feel some nervousness he would no longer be taking the exercise seriously. Another preacher suggested a practice which I have found helpful in combating nervousness and even occasionally feelings of over confidence. The suggestion is to focus on the task in hand.

The Church Service

I am aware that the title of this afterword is "The Art of Preaching" but it is rare indeed for a sermon to be in isolation from a service of worship. There are a number of churches which regularly follow a set ritual, such as the Catholic, Anglican and Orthodox which do not usually emphasise preaching. There may be a message but it is often called a "homily." As the ritual in these churches is set, the comments which follow apply more to churches such as Baptist,

Church of Christ, Pentecostal, Uniting which emphasise preaching in which the surrounding service may vary.

There is need for a note to suggest that churches of the variety just mentioned usually develop a certain practice as ritual is a natural part of life as a whole and of various gatherings. Throughout the centuries those who are a part of churches without a set ritual have often been critical of those who have this practice. Whatever approach a church has adopted one of the reasons people attend it is the familiarity they have with the approach used which brings, comfort and encouragement.

PREPARATION

The Prayers

Some of the evangelical tradition would find it anathema to consider preparing the prayers for a service. Their reasoning is that this interferes with inspiration. They feel that prayers should be extemporaneous, to prepare, smacks of ritual. My experience, first of all in my own early practice and in listening to countless prayers over the years, is that without preparation people drift into the use of the same phraseology and even topics and in addition are prone to pray at inordinate length.

Most services have the following prayers, Invocation (start of service), thanksgiving, dedication of offering, intercession (often called, "prayers of the people), petition. I will comment on each prayer but in any particular service, I believe there should be an effort to follow the chosen theme, as much as possible.

Invocation

It's become common, usually after words of welcome, to commence a service with a "call to worship." Quite often, the one leading the service will read all or part of the Psalm listed in the lectionary. Also quite often, the words of the Psalm are not really appropriate for a "call to worship." My own practice is to start the service with an

AFTERWORD

"Introduction to the Theme," the reason being that the congregation knows immediately the direction the service will or could take.

The Invocation can incorporate the theme and possibly commence with words such as "May we in this service . . .."

Prayers of Thanksgiving and Confession

Anyone reading this who is familiar with worship will probably wonder at the exclusion of "praise or adoration" with thanksgiving. This would be the most customary practice. My personal experience of such prayers indicates that leaders of worship can often get carried away with excessive verbiage as they express praise and adoration. Expressions of thanks are a highly valuable part of everyday life, but sadly, sometimes forgotten. Thanksgiving is much more easily related to the theme of the service. In this regard there may be particular aspects of the life and message of Jesus to include, or particular parts of the Bible, or the church as well as possible experiences of the wider community or particular individuals.

I think it necessary to include a note about the length of these prayers and the same will apply to "Prayers of intercession" later. Prayers which continue longer than 4 minutes maximum could be sleep producing. In churches in which the congregation in general may kneel, there is little conducement to sleep, but in those who may be subject to what has been called, "the protestant crouch" or bowing the head and closing eyes, there is every opportunity to lapse into sleep if the prayer is too long. Personally, to avoid this possibility I do not close my eyes in communal prayer. That confession has already brought me relief.

Prayers of Confession

Basing the prayers of confession on aspects of the theme give them some focus. Over the years, in this part of the service I have felt that the worship leader has at times, confessed things on my behalf which I don't feel guilty of. I have made it a practice of beginning the attitudes or deeds mentioned with the words, "If we have . . ." Many times the worship leader will follow the prayers of confession with an "assurance of forgiveness," usually quoting a verse of Scripture. Personally, after the confession I say, "As we accept forgiveness," followed by a brief prayer seeking change.

Offertory Prayer

After the offering is taken up it is brought forward and a prayer of dedication is offered. Personally I find this is the most difficult prayer to prepare as I like to make the effort to have some variety. Sometimes it is possible to tie the prayer into the theme. An example of a customary prayer is as follows, "Lord God, be pleased to accept these gifts, may they be wisely used in the extension of your Kingdom."

Prayers of Intercession (Prayers of the people)

As with the practice of choosing a theme for each service, when the Uniting Church came about, I discovered guidelines for the format of "prayers of intercession" in the preliminary orders of service for Holy Communion. The following categories for these prayers were suggested, "the church, peoples of the world, the community (I have taken that to mean, the local district—sometimes state and nation and also ones own church, those in need—at this point people in the congregation with particular needs are named (with their consent), shut ins, those in hospital." I conclude with a brief petition to do with our own following of the particular theme.

AN ONGOING PLEA IN CONCLUSION

The Church as a whole goes through troublous times. At least in developed nations, other than the current wave in Pentecostal type churches, the average congregation has dropped in numbers and has aged. Those theologians who have sought to adapt the timeless

Afterword

message to the contemporary scene such as "the process theologians" have produced interesting approaches. There has been a great deal of critical thought from those who often call themselves "progressives." Most times I believe they have rightly been critical of traditional theology and sometimes see little place for the church. The fact that I have called this afterword "The Art of Preaching" hopefully suggests that I am convinced that the church still has an important part to play in the spread of the teaching and attitudes of Jesus with emphasis on the main thrust of his message, the "Kingdom" or reign of God. The church service with what is in many churches the main part, the sermon, has a major role to play.

www.ingramcontent.com/pod-product-compliance
Lightning Source LLC
Chambersburg PA
CBHW071609170426
43196CB00034B/2246